Data-oriented Development with AngularJS

Write DSLs for your user interface code using AngularJS directives and add real-time capabilities to your applications using AngularFire's three-way data binding with Firebase

Manoj Waikar

PUBLISHING

BIRMINGHAM - MUMBAI

Data-oriented Development with AngularJS

First published: April 2015

Production reference: 1240415

Published by Packt Publishing Ltd.
Livery Place
35 Livery Street
Birmingham B3 2PB, UK.

ISBN 978-1-78439-805-7

www.packtpub.com

Credits

Author
Manoj Waikar

Reviewers
Mark Coleman
Pavlo Iuriichuk
Mourad Mourafiq
Arvind Ravulavaru

Commissioning Editor
Kunal Parikh

Acquisition Editor
Meeta Rajani

Content Development Editor
Arwa Manasawala

Technical Editor
Shruti Rawool

Copy Editors
Heeral Bhat
Pranjali Chury
Tani Kothari
Sonia Mathur
Karuna Narayanan
Kriti Sharma

Project Coordinator
Danuta Jones

Proofreaders
Simran Bhogal
Bridget Braund
Safis Editing

Indexer
Mariammal Chettiyar

Production Coordinator
Arvindkumar Gupta

Cover Work
Arvindkumar Gupta

About the Author

Manoj Waikar has been developing software for close to 15 years now. He started writing desktop applications in VB6 and has used almost all of the .NET and C# versions to write enterprise software. His urge to improve his craft led him to explore, and eventually use, open source frameworks such as NHibernate, Spring.NET, NUnit, Moq, and so on, which, until a few years ago, were not commonly used in the .NET world.

He admires RoR (Ruby on Rails) and thanks Microsoft for ASP.NET MVC and Web API. Due to some of the limitations of server-side MVC frameworks, he introduced AngularJS in one of the UK-based start-ups that he worked with and used it to great success.

He is interested in functional programming and loves Clojure (a Lisp for the JVM) and ClojureScript (which compiles to JavaScript). Of late, he has also started exploring F# and considers it the best language for the .NET platform.

Acknowledgments

First and foremost, I would like to thank my wife, Aboli, for always being there for me and my family. Although I piss her off sometimes with my incessant questions, I admire her decision-making skills and insightful answers. Hopefully, I'll learn from her one day. She even let me take almost a year off from work while she was the earning partner. I hope to return the favor soon. Thanks also to my kids for being patient with me while I was writing and for doing their own studies too—I'll certainly spend more time with them after this book is done.

I am lucky to have not just loving and supportive parents but also a caring and trustworthy extended family, because of my upbringing in a joint family (which is rare these days). Life would certainly be less fun without my uncles, aunts, and dear cousins. Thanks to my many friends for sharing their good (and bad) thoughts, learning, and insights.

Thanks are also due to all my teachers from the schools and colleges I attended for sharing their knowledge and making me capable in this journey of life. Special thanks to my illustrious uncle, Dr. Ganesh Tarey, for teaching me mathematics and physics (the two dreaded subjects) and my brilliant cousin, Anil Bhatnagar, for teaching me many fun math techniques—I started liking math and computers because of you both.

Countless thanks to the creators/maintainers and contributors of excellent open source software/languages/frameworks—software development would be utterly boring without your selfless efforts. Thanks also to all the wonderful authors from whose books I've learned so much—finishing a book is such a Herculean effort in itself.

Thanks to Packt Publishing for giving me the chance to become an author and the entire team at Packt Publishing who endured with me throughout this journey. Special thanks to Meeta Rajani, Arwa Manasawala, and Shruti Rawool for being patient with me and pushing me gently to finish chapter after chapter. This book wouldn't be in your hands without their efforts and help.

My sincerest and heartfelt thanks to the reviewers: Mark, Pavlo, Mourad, and Arvind. They not only pointed out some errors in the code, but also gave excellent suggestions to improve the code and the content. This book is in a much better shape because of you all.

Thanks to the entire IDFC team at Indus software, where I learned the tricks of the trade. Thanks to HCL technologies for my first ever trip to USA and also to the entire team at SunGard Offshore Services, Pune, India, and SunGard Investran, USA, with whom I've spent some fruitful years of my career. I would also like to thank my entire team at PJM Interconnection, USA, for one of the best projects and probably the best work culture. Last but not least, thanks to Intelliheads Technology and my boss, Daniel Niasoff, for letting us use AngularJS — you are the root cause of this book.

About the Reviewers

Mark Coleman is a full-stack developer focusing on the latest in web technologies. He enjoys learning about new technologies. He also likes to share his knowledge by attending local development groups and blogging (www.kramnameloc.com) about programming topics. When Mark is not absorbing everything to do with development, he enjoys photography and anything pertaining to The Simpsons and is a part-time craft beer/bacon aficionado.

Pavlo Iuriichuk is a frontend lead developer who works at GlobalLogic and has about 7 years of frontend development experience on various platforms, including those on mobile and desktop. He graduated from Kyiv Polytechnic Institute 5 years ago with a master diploma in applied mathematics.

He has previously worked for various outsourcing companies in Ukraine, including Ciklum, Cybervisiontech, and 2K-group.

Previously, he has reviewed *HTML5 and CSS3 Transition, Transformation, and Animation*, *Packt Publishing*.

I want to thank my team and friends who encouraged me to review this book that they will use to improve their in-depth skills in frontend technologies.

Mourad Mourafiq is a software engineer and data scientist. After successfully completing his studies in applied mathematics, he worked in an investment bank as a quantitative modeler in the structured products market, specializing in ABS, CDO, and CDS, after which he worked as a quantitative analyst for the largest bank in France.

After a couple of years in the financial world, he developed a passion for machine learning and computational mathematics, and decided to join a start-up that specialized in software mining and artificial intelligence.

He was also involved in reviewing *Python for Finance* and *Getting Started with Python pandas*, both by Packt Publishing.

Arvind Ravulavaru is a full-stack consultant with over 6 years of experience in software development. For the last 2 years, he has been working extensively on JavaScript, both on the server and client side. In his spare time, Arvind likes to experiment with new and upcoming technologies. He also blogs at http://thejackalofjavascript.com.

I would like to thank my family, especially my mother, for making all this happen!

www.PacktPub.com

Support files, eBooks, discount offers, and more

For support files and downloads related to your book, please visit www.PacktPub.com.

Did you know that Packt offers eBook versions of every book published, with PDF and ePub files available? You can upgrade to the eBook version at www.PacktPub.com and as a print book customer, you are entitled to a discount on the eBook copy. Get in touch with us at service@packtpub.com for more details.

At www.PacktPub.com, you can also read a collection of free technical articles, sign up for a range of free newsletters and receive exclusive discounts and offers on Packt books and eBooks.

https://www2.packtpub.com/books/subscription/packtlib

Do you need instant solutions to your IT questions? PacktLib is Packt's online digital book library. Here, you can search, access, and read Packt's entire library of books.

Why subscribe?

- Fully searchable across every book published by Packt
- Copy and paste, print, and bookmark content
- On demand and accessible via a web browser

Free access for Packt account holders

If you have an account with Packt at www.PacktPub.com, you can use this to access PacktLib today and view 9 entirely free books. Simply use your login credentials for immediate access.

To my mother, late Mrs. Usha Waikar

Table of Contents

Preface

If you've ever wanted to create database-backed Single Page Applications (SPAs), this book will show you how to do it using the power of AngularJS. Along the way, you'll also learn the best practices of AngularJS development and will see how to structure your frontend code that greatly improves maintainability. You'll also learn how to create custom controls using AngularJS directives.

If you've ever wondered how to write applications that update data in real time without refreshing your browsers or without employing server-side push technologies, then this book shows you how easy it is using Firebase and AngularFire. Firebase resembles the document-oriented NoSQL stores, so you'll also learn how to structure your data in Firebase. Finally, you'll use Firebase's anonymous authentication and other best practices learned along the way in a hands-on example application.

What this book covers

Chapter 1, *AngularJS Rationale and Data Binding*, talks about why AngularJS is needed and why you should choose AngularJS over other client-side/server-side frameworks. It also talks about data binding, shows a simple Hello World application, and an application that demonstrates two-way data binding.

Chapter 2, *Working with Data*, talks about the whys and hows of dependency injection in Angular. Then it talks about filters and promises and finally shows you how to do Ajax communication using $http and $resource services.

Chapter 3, *Custom Controls*, is all about directives. It shows how you can write custom elements, attributes, and so on, and also talks about isolate scopes, transclusion, and other stuff about directives.

Chapter 4, Firebase, talks about different types of persistence mechanisms and local versus hosted databases. It then talks about the value proposition of Firebase and discusses AngularFire. Finally, it shows how to structure data while using Firebase and also talks about denormalization.

Chapter 5, Getting Started with AngularFire, shows how to use AngularFire. It shows synchronized objects and arrays and also shows three-way data binding in action.

Chapter 6, Applied Angular and AngularFire, builds an example application that shows how to use Firebase's anonymous authentication. It shows the difference between Angular factory and service, which is a commonly confused topic. It also uses Angular best practices in the example application.

Appendix A, Yeoman, demonstrates the use of yo (for scaffolding), grunt, and gulp (for building) and bower (for dependency management) tools. It discusses the advantage of using these tools and also shows how to install them using Node Package Manager (NPM).

Appendix B, Git and Git Flow, introduces Git which is one of the most widely used version control systems today. It shows the most basic Git commands to help you get started with Git quickly. It also shows simple Git branching and merging, and introduces Git flow – a tool which prescribes a practical branching model and makes branching and merging a joy.

Appendix C, Editors and IDEs, talks about editors and IDEs that have good support for web (HTML, CSS, and JavaScript) development technologies. The obvious candidates are Visual Studio, Eclipse, and Sublime Text and oldies such as Emacs and Vim. It also highlights the support for AngularJS in Brackets (backed by Adobe) and WebStorm (by JetBrains).

What you need for this book

All that you need for the examples in this book is a good text editor that has support for HTML/JavaScript syntax highlighting and any modern PC/Laptop.

Who this book is for

This book helps beginner-level AngularJS developers to organize AngularJS applications by discussing important AngularJS concepts and best practices. If you are an experienced AngularJS developer, but haven't yet written directives or created custom HTML controls, then this book is ideal for you. This book also shows you how to build real-time apps using Firebase/AngularFire to store and sync data in real time.

Conventions

In this book, you will find a number of text styles that distinguish between different kinds of information. Here are some examples of these styles and an explanation of their meaning.

Code words in text, database table names, folder names, filenames, file extensions, pathnames, dummy URLs, user input, and Twitter handles are shown as follows: "We loaded the `ngRoute` module as a dependent of the `routeApp` module."

A block of code is set as follows:

```
'use strict';
app.service('employeeSvc', function () {

  var Employee = function (name, age) {
    this.name = name;
    this.age = age;
  };

Var getEmployees = function () {
    return [
      new Employee("First employee", 56),
      new Employee("Second employee", 44),
      new Employee("Last employee", 32)
    ];
  };

  // Public API
  this.Employee = Employee;
  this.getEmployees = getEmployees;
});
```

When we wish to draw your attention to a particular part of a code block, the relevant lines or items are set in bold:

```
<br>
<div>
  <h1>Employee data:</h1>
  <ul>
    <li ng-repeat="employee in employeeData.employees">
      Employee - {{employee.name}} is - {{employee.age}} years old
    </li>
  </ul>
</div>
```

Any command-line input or output is written as follows:

```
bower install underscore
```

New terms and **important words** are shown in bold. Words that you see on the screen, for example, in menus or dialog boxes, appear in the text like this: "For other extensions, the **Install** button is enabled."

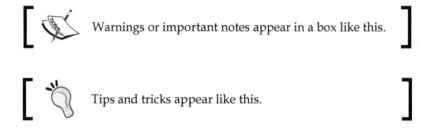

Warnings or important notes appear in a box like this.

Tips and tricks appear like this.

Reader feedback

Feedback from our readers is always welcome. Let us know what you think about this book—what you liked or disliked. Reader feedback is important for us as it helps us develop titles that you will really get the most out of.

To send us general feedback, simply e-mail feedback@packtpub.com, and mention the book's title in the subject of your message.

If there is a topic that you have expertise in and you are interested in either writing or contributing to a book, see our author guide at www.packtpub.com/authors.

Customer support

Now that you are the proud owner of a Packt book, we have a number of things to help you to get the most from your purchase.

Downloading the example code

You can download the example code files from your account at http://www.packtpub.com for all the Packt Publishing books you have purchased. If you purchased this book elsewhere, you can visit http://www.packtpub.com/support and register to have the files e-mailed directly to you.

Errata

Although we have taken every care to ensure the accuracy of our content, mistakes do happen. If you find a mistake in one of our books—maybe a mistake in the text or the code—we would be grateful if you could report this to us. By doing so, you can save other readers from frustration and help us improve subsequent versions of this book. If you find any errata, please report them by visiting http://www.packtpub.com/submit-errata, selecting your book, clicking on the **Errata Submission Form** link, and entering the details of your errata. Once your errata are verified, your submission will be accepted and the errata will be uploaded to our website or added to any list of existing errata under the Errata section of that title.

To view the previously submitted errata, go to https://www.packtpub.com/books/content/support and enter the name of the book in the search field. The required information will appear under the **Errata** section.

Piracy

Piracy of copyrighted material on the Internet is an ongoing problem across all media. At Packt, we take the protection of our copyright and licenses very seriously. If you come across any illegal copies of our works in any form on the Internet, please provide us with the location address or website name immediately so that we can pursue a remedy.

Please contact us at copyright@packtpub.com with a link to the suspected pirated material.

We appreciate your help in protecting our authors and our ability to bring you valuable content.

Questions

If you have a problem with any aspect of this book, you can contact us at questions@packtpub.com, and we will do our best to address the problem.

1
AngularJS Rationale and Data Binding

AngularJS is described as a "Superheroic JavaScript MVW Framework" (where **MVW** stands for **Model-View-Whatever**). Google search's content description for AngularJS is as follows:

> "*AngularJS is what HTML would have been, had it been designed for building web-apps. Declarative templates with data-binding, MVW, MVVM, MVC, dependency injection, and great testability story all implemented with pure client-side JavaScript!*"

 MVVM is a pattern used in building **Windows Presentation Foundation (WPF)** applications. A ViewModel represents the model for the view and is bound to various UI elements. This is called **data binding**. Typically, if the ViewModel changes, the UI elements update themselves, and if a value is changed in any of the UI elements (because of user interaction or otherwise), the underlying ViewModel gets updated. This is called **two-way data binding**. This is a very powerful concept, as we'll see in the later chapters. The developer does not have to update the UI whenever there is a change in the ViewModel and vice versa. This two-way data binding leads to the elimination of a lot of boilerplate code.

So, what do we gain by having MVVM and MVC in the same framework? As explained earlier, MVVM gives AngularJS the data binding power, and MVC helps you build applications that follow a clean separation of concerns. Testing monolithic applications is very difficult. MVC gives a proper structure to your applications, and different components can be tested individually.

Since AngularJS supports MVC and MVVM architectural patterns, it's described as the MVW (Model-View-Whatever) or MV* framework.

 AngularJS or Angular (for brevity) will be used interchangeably in this book.

In this chapter, we will:

- Compare and contrast frameworks and libraries
- Compare and contrast Angular with server-side MVC frameworks
- Compare and contrast Angular with other client-side MVC frameworks
- Find out why to choose Angular over other alternatives
- Learn about data binding (and two-way data binding)
- Learn how to bind a collection of data
- Find out some naming conventions and learn how to organize Angular applications

Frameworks versus libraries

You have two choices to aid your development efforts—either choose a framework like Rails or AngularJS or choose smaller libraries. The Clojure community (in general) dislikes frameworks, so there wasn't a full-fledged web framework such as Rails in the Clojure landscape for long. Let's look at the pros and cons of choosing one over the other:

Frameworks	Libraries
Pros	
Less R&D is needed: A framework will solve a lot of problems, and you won't need as many libraries to get the work done.	**Smaller learning curve**: A library is typically easier to learn than a framework.
Better code quality: Since the framework has a prescribed way of doing things, you can follow the prescribed best practices and your code will attain a much better quality (than if you were to do things yourself).	**Easier to fix library bugs**: It might be easier to fix a bug in the library itself (because of the smaller codebase).

Frameworks	Libraries
Uniformity in code: Different codebases written using the same framework are easier to understand. This is because they all will be following the same structure, patterns, and so on.	**More flexible**: Since you're choosing libraries, it might be easier to adapt those individual libraries to your needs.
Cons	
Bigger learning curve: Depending on what a framework does, it can be big or small and the learning curve will be proportionately large or small.	**More R&D is needed**: Since you'll have to use many libraries to complete your task, you'll have to spend time and resources to research many different libraries.
Code complexity: The code will be more complex for anyone who hasn't learned the ways of the framework.	**Code quality**: Since you are using many different libraries, you might have to come up with ways to organize code. Consequently, the code quality might suffer (this is less of a problem for experienced developers).
Less flexible: Any task for which there is a prescribed way of doing things is easy to implement. However, it may prove to be difficult to implement tasks outside the purview of the framework.	**Missing uniformity in code**: Two developers using the same library might structure code in totally different ways. Alternatively, two codebases that use the same set of libraries might be structured in a totally different way. So, there are less chances of code uniformity between two different codebases.
Difficult to fix framework bugs: It might be difficult to fix bugs in the framework itself.	**Learning curve**: It might be easier to learn a library. However, if you are trying to replace a framework, chances are that you'll have to learn about various libraries. So, the learning curve might be higher than learning a single framework.

AngularJS versus server-side MVC frameworks

So, why should one choose a client-side JavaScript MVC framework over other server-side frameworks, such as Rails or Asp.Net MVC? Typically, the controller methods of any server-side MVC framework return views (that is, a fully formed HTML). However, there are cases when a view needs some data through Ajax calls (for obvious reasons). In such cases, the question arises as to which controller (method) should send this data. This leads to complexities on two fronts, which are described here:

- **The view becomes complex**: In this case, you have to understand not only the part of the view that is generated by the server, but also all the AJAX interactions happening on the view. Then, you have to decide where to include the JavaScript code related to the view — in the same view in script tags or in a separate JavaScript file. Often, a server-side MVC framework uses a different template engine to build the HTML. This problem can be mitigated using a template engine such as Handlebars (`http://handlebarsjs.com/`).

 Ideally, the syntax of the template engine should be close to the actual HTML syntax. This is so that when the designers give developers an updated HTML design, it becomes easy to incorporate their changes.

- **The controller becomes complex**: Some of the controller methods return complete views, while others return data. If you are using a client-side MV* framework, then the server-side controllers are API controllers, which only send data to the client. It is up to the client to display the data in whichever way it pleases. This makes the controllers simpler.

Similarly, the client-side MV* framework itself gives you some well-defined mechanisms to organize your code as per the MVC paradigm (or whatever convention the framework wants you to follow). So, the view code also becomes simpler and organized. Moreover, every interaction of the view with the server happens through Ajax calls. This too brings uniformity of communication.

AngularJS versus other frontend JavaScript frameworks

While researching for frontend JavaScript frameworks, you'll realize that there are four main open-source contenders: AngularJS, Backbone (`http://backbonejs.org/`), Ember (`http://emberjs.com/`), and, the latest kid on the block, React from Facebook (`http://facebook.github.io/react/`).

Sure, there is jQuery, but it is a library used mainly for DOM manipulations, event handling, and Ajax communication. Similarly, Knockout (`http://knockoutjs.com/`) is a small framework/library that provides data binding, which greatly simplifies dynamic JavaScript UIs with the MVVM pattern. Likewise, React only caters to the View layer (V in MVC) and isn't a full MVC framework.

However, for a large-scale, database-backed web application, you'll need more than what libraries such as jQuery or Knockout provide. I have no experience with Backbone, Ember, or React, so here are a few links that will help you compare them:

- *Angular Backbone or Ember: Which is best for your Build?* (`https://www.codeschool.com/blog/2014/05/15/angular-backbone-or-ember-which-is-best-for-your/`)

- *Angular Backbone Ember: The best JavaScript framework for you* (`http://readwrite.com/2014/02/06/angular-backbone-ember-best-javascript-framework-for-you`)

- *Backbone and Angular: Demystifying the myths* (`http://blog.nebithi.com/backbone-and-angular-demystifying-the-myths/`)

Why AngularJS?

So, this begs the question, "Why should you choose AngularJS?" The choice of framework depends on a lot of factors—sometimes even personal preferences play a role in deciding a framework. However, let's look at some of the technical and pragmatic reasons that justify choosing AngularJS over other frameworks:

- **Documentation**: Google maintains an excellent and in-depth documentation for AngularJS at `https://docs.angularjs.org/api`.

- **Books**: There is a wealth of excellent books on AngularJS, such as *Mastering Web Application Development with AngularJS* (`https://www.packtpub.com/web-development/mastering-web-application-development-angularjs`), *Mastering AngularJS Directives* (`https://www.packtpub.com/application-development/mastering-angularjs-directives`), and many others.

- **Data binding**: With two-way data binding, when you update the DOM, your model gets updated and vice versa. This leads to code reduction.

- **POJO**: Plain old JavaScript objects can be used for data binding. You don't need any special syntax to achieve data binding.

- **The $http service**: This simplifies Ajax communication.

- **The $resource service**: This provides a higher level abstraction than the `$http` service. This service is used to communicate with RESTful APIs.

- **HTTP interceptors**: For purposes of global error handling, authentication, or any kind of synchronous or asynchronous preprocessing of request or postprocessing of responses, we can use HTTP interceptors.

- **Directives**: This is a complex but very powerful feature of AngularJS. This feature (`https://www.packtpub.com/application-development/mastering-angularjs-directives`) is the one that "teaches old HTML, some new tricks". Using directives, you can build custom HTML elements, attributes, and so on.

- **Dependency injection**: Most of the server-side object-oriented languages have dependency-injection support available through some library/framework. You can expect the same ease of use with AngularJS's built-in support for dependency injection in your favorite language—JavaScript.

- **Unit testing support**: This is a must when developing with a dynamic language such as JavaScript. AngularJS has excellent support for unit testing—it comes with mocks for a number of its built-in services.

- **Support**: AngularJS is backed by none other than Google. It becomes easy to convince your boss if a company like Google is behind a framework or technology.

- **Community**: This plays an important role when you are learning something new. There are already a lot of questions answered on sites such as StackOverflow (`http://stackoverflow.com/`). You'll find many more resources on Twitter and many other websites.

- **Companion frameworks**: Ionic (`http://ionicframework.com/`) is a frontend framework to develop hybrid mobile apps with HTML5. This framework is optimized for AngularJS.

Data binding

Data binding is the process that establishes a connection between the application UI and data. So, data binding has two participants: the **model** (or the getter and setter properties of the model) and the **UI element** (to which the model is bound). In the case of AngularJS, the UI elements are the various DOM elements that make up our UI.

When the data changes its value, the UI elements that are bound to the data reflect changes automatically. Conversely, when the data shown in the UI element changes, the underlying model is updated to reflect the changes.

AngularJS Hello World!

Every programming language has a venerable Hello World code example that forms the starting point in the study of that language. So, how can AngularJS be left behind?

The following is AngularJS's *Hello World* example. This example shows data binding in action:

```
<!DOCTYPE html>
<html>
<head>
  <script src="https://ajax.googleapis.com/ajax/libs/angularjs/1.3.0-
beta.17/angular.min.js"></script>
  <title>Hello world from AngularJS</title>
</head>
<body>
  <div ng-app>
    <div>
      <label>Name:</label>
      <input type="text" ng-model="yourName" placeholder="Enter a
      name here">
      <hr>
      <h1>Hello {{yourName}}!</h1>
    </div>
  </div>
</body>
</html>
```

(hello-world.html)

Let's take a look at the preceding code (especially the highlighted parts of the code):

- Inside the script tag, we included a reference to `angular.min.js`.

- The `ngApp` directive is used to autobootstrap an AngularJS application. This directive is a part of the `ng` core module. The `ng` module is loaded by default when an AngularJS application is started. The `ngApp` directive designates the root element of the application. Whenever Angular finds the ngApp directive, it loads the module associated with the directive. From this point on, Angular can start its magic. This directive is typically placed near the root element of the page, for example, on the `<body>` or `<html>` tags. Alternatively, it can be placed on the part of the HTML that we want AngularJS to control.

  - **Directives**: These are markers on a DOM element (such as an attribute, element name, comment, or CSS class). They tell AngularJS's HTML compiler to attach a specified behavior to that DOM element or even transform the DOM element and its children. You can read more about directives in the AngularJS directive guide at `https://docs.angularjs.org/guide/directive`. Also, notice that the names of the AngularJS directives we've used so far are `ngApp` and `ngModel`, whereas in the HTML document, we are using `ng-app` and `ng-model`. By convention, directives are named using camelCase in JavaScript and snake case within your HTML. Snake case means all lowercase, using either `:`, `-`, or `_` to separate the words. So, `ng-app` can also be written as `ng_app` or `ng:app`.

  - **Bootstrapping**: This is the Angular initialization process and can be done in one of two ways: automatic initialization (which is the recommended way) or manual initialization (in cases when you need to perform an operation before Angular compiles a page). The automatic initialization process, as explained above, starts when Angular encounters an ngApp directive. You can read more about the AngularJS bootstrap process in the AngularJS bootstrap guide available at `https://docs.angularjs.org/guide/bootstrap`.

- The `ngModel` directive binds `input`, `select`, and `textarea` (or custom form control) to a property on the scope.

  - **Scope** refers to the application model and acts as the glue between application controller and the view. You can read more about scopes in the AngularJS scope guide at `https://docs.angularjs.org/guide/scope`.

- `{{yourName}}` renders the value of this variable in the DOM element. It means whatever value was stored in the `yourName` variable is extracted and displayed in the enclosing DOM element.

- So, in short, we created a `yourName` variable on the scope and bound it to the input element (which means, the data entered in the input box is stored in this variable). Then, we just showed the value of the `yourName` variable in the `h1` element. So, as soon as you start typing into the input textbox, you'll see the same text reflected in the `h1` element. This is **one-way data binding** in action. Isn't it cool!

You'll also notice that there are no IDs assigned to any of the HTML elements! This is possible because of the power of data binding—you'll hardly need to retrieve a DOM element based on its ID because data-bound properties on the scope will do the magic.

Two-way data binding

Let's extend the preceding example to illustrate two-way data binding:

```
<!DOCTYPE html>
<html>
<head>
  <script src="https://ajax.googleapis.com/ajax/libs/angularjs/
    1.3.0-beta.17/angular.min.js"></script>
  <title>AngularJS - Two way data binding</title>
</head>
<body>
  <div ng-app>
    <div>
      <h2 style="color:blue;">One way data binding? Cool!</h2>
      <label>Name:</label>
      <input type="text" ng-model="yourName" placeholder="Enter a
        name here">
      <h3>Hello {{yourName}}!</h3>
    </div>
    <hr />
    <div>
      <h2 style="color:green;">Two way data binding? Great!</h2>
      <textarea type="text" ng-model="newName" placeholder="Enter
        some text to change the value of the underlying
        model"></textarea>
      <button ng-click="yourName = newName">
        Change the underlying model's value
      </button>
    </div>
  </div>
</body>
</html>
```

(`two-way-data-binding.html`)

- We've made very few changes to our preceding Hello World example. We introduced a `<textarea>` element and bound it to a new model variable called `newName`.

- We added a `<button>` element, and we are handling its clicked event (using the `ngClick` directive). Inside the click event, we just assigned the value of the `newName` new model to our old variable `yourName`.

- As soon as you enter some text in the `textarea` value and click on the **Change the underlying model's value** button, the `textarea` value is reflected in the **Name** textbox and the **Hello** label.

- This shows two-way data binding in action. The UI control reflects the value of the underlying model and vice versa.

Collection binding

Let's see how to bind data when we have a collection (or a list) of values. For clarity, we'll only show the important part of the code.

```html
<body ng-app="collectionBindingApp">
  <div ng-controller="EmployeeCtrl">
    <h1>Employee data:</h1>
    In a list -
    <ul>
      <li ng-repeat="employee in employeeData.employees">
        Employee number {{$index}} is - {{employee.name}}
      </li>
    </ul>

    <br />In a table -
    <table>
      <tr>
        <th>Name</th>
        <th>Age</th>
      </tr>
      <tr ng-repeat="employee in employeeData.employees">
        <td>{{employee.name}}</td>
        <td>{{employee.age}}</td>
      </tr>
    </table>
  </div>

  <script src="app.js"></script>
</body>
```

(`collection-binding-ex\index.html`)

You're now familiar with the `ng-app` directive. AngularJS starts its magic from this point onwards. We then attach `EmployeeCtrl` to the `div` element using the `ng-controller` directive. The `ng-repeat` directive instantiates a template once per item in the collection, which is `employeeData.employees` here. So, in the first instance in the preceding code, it repeats the `<li>` elements, whereas in the second case, it repeats the `<tr>` elements. Each template instance gets its own scope, and `$index` is set to the item index or key.

Let's look at the controller now (again, for clarity, we are showing a part of the code):

```javascript
var app = angular.module('collectionBindingApp', []);

app.controller('EmployeeCtrl', ['$scope',
  function ($scope) {

    var Employee = function (name, age) {
      this.name = name;
      this.age = age;
    };

    var getEmployees = function () {
      return [
        new Employee("First employee", 56),
        new Employee("Second employee", 44),
        new Employee("Last employee", 32)
      ];
    };

    $scope.employeeData = {
      employees: getEmployees()
    };
  }
]);
```

(`collection-binding-ex\app.js`)

Downloading the example code

You can download the example code files from your account at `http://www.packtpub.com` for all the Packt Publishing books you have purchased. If you purchased this book elsewhere, you can visit `http://www.packtpub.com/support` and register to have the files e-mailed directly to you.

We first create a new module called `collectionBindingApp` using the below API :

```
angular.module(name, [requires], [configFn]);
```

Here `name` is the name of the module to create or retrieve. The second argument is optional — if it is specified then a new module is being created, else an existing module is being retrieved for further configuration. The third parameter is an optional configuration function for the module.

We store the module in the `app` variable. This `app` variable is available globally and is used to associate controllers, directives, filters, and so on with this module. Then we create a controller called `EmployeeCtrl` on this new module.

We should use a controller to set up the initial state of the `$scope` object and to add behavior to the `$scope` object. We declared our new controller, called `EmployeeCtrl`, and associate it with the `collectionBindingApp` module. This controller has a few functions to generate test data, but in real-life scenarios, you'll typically fetch data from RESTful services (for which you can use the `$http` service or the `$resource` service). So, we set the state here by assigning some employees to the `$scope.employeeData` object. An advantage of using an object is that you don't clutter `$scope` with too many variables. So, when you run the example, you see the employee data, first in a list (which also shows the index) and then in a tabular form.

It would've become pretty obvious by now that data binding can reduce a lot of DOM manipulation code from the application and is a powerful technique. AngularJS brings data-binding capabilities within the realm of web applications. We can use it in our favorite platform, that is, the Web, HTML5, and JavaScript.

Routes

The `ngRoute` (`https://docs.angularjs.org/api/ngRoute`) module and the `ngView` (`https://docs.angularjs.org/api/ngRoute/directive/ngView`) directive are the secret sauces that let us write **Single Page Applications (SPAs)** with ease. We configure which views are to be shown for which URLs using the `$routeProvider` service. This service comes with the `ngRoute` module. This module comes with the `angular-route.js` library, so we have to include it separately. So, let's see them in action:

```
<!DOCTYPE html>
<html>

<head>
  <script src="https://ajax.googleapis.com/ajax/libs/angularjs/
    1.3.14/angular.min.js"></script>
```

```
    <script src="https://ajax.googleapis.com/ajax/libs/angularjs/
      1.3.14/angular-route.min.js"></script>
    <title>Routing example</title>
  </head>

  <body ng-app="routeApp">
    Choose:<br><br>
    <a href="#employees">Employees</a><br>
    <a href="#departments">Departments</a>

    <div ng-view></div>

    <script src="app.js"></script>
    <script src="employee.ctl.js"></script>
    <script src="department.ctl.js"></script>
  </body>

</html>
```

(route-ex/index.html)

First, we included the angular-route.min.js library. Then, as usual, we set up a routeApp module and then we set up two links—one each to navigate to employees and departments. Note that the links have a leading # because we don't want the browser to actually navigate to the employees.html or departments.html page. Finally, we added the ng-view directive to our div element, which works together with the $route service. It serves as the placeholder where the HTML contents of various templates are rendered as per the current route. Hence, it includes the rendered template of the current route into the main layout (index.html). The configuration of routes is done in the following app.js file:

```
var app = angular.module('routeApp', [
  'ngRoute'
]);

app.config(function ($routeProvider) {
  $routeProvider
    .when('/employees', {
      templateUrl: 'employee.tpl.html',
      controller: 'EmployeeCtrl'
    })
    .when('/departments', {
      templateUrl: 'department.tpl.html',
      controller: 'DepartmentCtrl'
    })
```

```
        .otherwise({
          redirectTo: '/'
        });
    });
```

(route-ex/app.js)

We loaded the `ngRoute` module as a dependent of the `routeApp` module. Next, we configured various routes of the module using `$routeProvider`. Here, we are saying that whenever the URL matches `/employees`, the `employee.tpl.html` template should be inserted in the `ng-view` placeholder of the `index.html` file with `EmployeeCtrl` as the controller. This also applies to the `/department` URL.

The `EmployeeCtrl` controller in `route-ex/employee.ctl.js` is similar to the one in the previous example, and `DepartmentCtrl` in `route-ex/department.ctl.js` mimics it. The templates for employee view and department view are also similar, as shown here:

```
<br>
<div>
  <h1>Employee data:</h1>
  <ul>
    <li ng-repeat="employee in employeeData.employees">
      Employee - {{employee.name}} is - {{employee.age}} years old
    </li>
  </ul>
</div>
```

(route-ex/employee.tpl.html)

Just as the employee template in the preceding code shows employee data, the department template shows department data. When you run the application and click on the employee link, you see the employee data, and ditto for the department link, without any page refreshes. Although this is a simple example, you can see how easy Angular makes it to write SPAs.

Other AngularJS directives

Other AngularJS directives such as `ngShow`, `ngHide`, `ngChecked`, and `ngSelected` are among the various other directives that help us in building great-looking UIs with minimal DOM manipulation code. AngularJS API docs (`https://docs.angularjs.org/api`) is a great place for exploring various directives, services etc. that Angular provides.

Organizing AngularJS applications

The success of a project can be judged not only by the timely delivery of working code but also by other factors such as:

- How much of the code is covered by tests
- How well organized the codebase is (in a proper folder structure)
- How consistent the naming convention is
- How easy it is for someone who is new to the project to understand the code

The naming conventions and many other factors are a matter of personal taste. However, for the sake of consistency, it's always advisable to agree on certain naming conventions and best practices to be followed for any important projects.

As discussed in *Appendix A, Yeoman*, tools such as Yeoman (`http://yeoman.io/`) help with the scaffolding and setting up of the initial folder structure. Similarly, code beautifiers available in various IDEs help in arranging the code in a single file to follow accepted norms with spaces, tabs, new lines, and so on.

You've got a taste of some of the naming conventions that I've followed in the preceding examples. For example, the template file has been named with a `.tpl.html` extension. Similarly, a controller file is named with a `.ctl.js` extension. Although it's a trivial change, it adds a lot to the overall code readability. Similarly, the names of the controllers starts with a capital letter (`EmployeeCtrl`), whereas the names of all other components start with a small letter (`collectionBindingApp`).

Yeoman organizes the code *by type*, that is, it has folders for controllers, views, services, and so on. This is OK at the beginning but has a distinct disadvantage: the files that logically belong together to a feature, that is, a view, a controller, and various services the controller needs, are in different folders. So, it becomes difficult to locate these files. When you are working on a particular feature, you are going to need these files at the same time.

So, the other option is to organize the code *by feature* or *by component*. So, assuming that your project deals with employees, departments, and so on, there will be folders named employees or departments. Views, controllers, services, and directives belonging to a component live in the particular component's folder.

You may refer to the following links for more details on organizing the Angular code:

- AngularJS style guide at `https://github.com/mgechev/angularjs-style-guide`
- AngularJS best practices at `https://github.com/GrumpyWizards/Angular`

- Best practices recommendations for Angular App structure at `https://docs.google.com/document/d/1XXMvReO8-Awi1EZXAXS4PzDzdNvV6pGcuaF4Q9821Es/pub`

- The Google JavaScript style guide at `http://google-styleguide.googlecode.com/svn/trunk/javascriptguide.xml`; this is a good place for general JavaScript conventions

Check out AngularJS Batarang (`https://chrome.google.com/webstore/detail/angularjs-batarang/ighdmehidhipcmcojjgiloacoafjmpfk?hl=en`), a Chrome extension. This helps in debugging JavaScript applications written using AngularJS. It gets added as an extra AngularJS tab in the developer tools where it shows different scopes and models. We can check which models are attached to which scope.

Also, check out Built with AngularJS (`https://builtwith.angularjs.org/`) for interesting examples of sites/applications built using AngularJS.

Summary

In this chapter, we compared and contrasted frameworks versus libraries, Angular versus the server-side MVC frameworks, and Angular versus the other client-side JS MVC frameworks. We also looked at some of the important reasons as to why we should choose Angular. Then, we talked about data binding and why and how it's powerful and consequently leads to reduction of code. Finally, we looked at a few of the naming conventions and how to organize Angular applications.

In the next chapter, we'll learn about advanced Angular concepts such as IoC and filters. You'll also learn how to fetch data using the `$http` and `$resource` services.

2
Working with Data

Now that we've already covered the basics of AngularJS and data binding, let's take a deep dive into Angular and see what dependency injection is, why it is needed, and how to do dependency injection in Angular. We'll also see the role of filters and how to write custom filters. Then, we'll see how to call remote APIs using the $http service and the $resource service. Finally, we'll study how the $resource service is an abstraction on top of the $http service and how it makes communication with RESTful APIs easier. So, let's get started.

In this chapter, we will cover the following topics:

- Dependency injection and why it is needed
- How dependency injection is achieved in Angular
- The role of filters and how to implement them
- What are promises?
- How to communicate with backend APIs using the $http service
- How the $resource service makes communication with RESTful services easier

Dependency injection

The dependency injection pattern, as the name suggests, is the process of injecting dependencies (or services) into another (client) object. It is also referred to as **Inversion of Control (IoC)**. Without it, a client has to create instances of dependent objects itself, whereas with dependency injection, these objects are handed to the client by someone else (typically, an IoC container). This is commonly referred to as the Hollywood principle—"don't call us, we'll call you". The following is an example C# code to make things more clear:

```csharp
public interface IShippingService {
  double CalculateShippingCost ();
}


public class ShippingService : IShippingService {
  double CalculateShippingCost () {
    // do some lengthy calculation here and
    // calculate the shipping cost
  }
}

public class LoggingShippingService : IShippingService {
  double CalculateShippingCost () {
    // do some lengthy calculation here and
    // calculate the shipping cost
    Console.WriteLine("Now log the cost");
  }
}

public class Client {
  // without IoC
  private IShippingService _shippingService;

  Client() {
    _shippingService = new ShippingService();
  }

  public ShowShippingCost() {
    Console.WriteLine("The total shipping cost is {0}",
      _shippingService.CalculateShippingCost());
  }
}
```

In the preceding code, the `Client` class needs an object of `ShippingService` to do its work. However, it creates an object of `ShippingService` itself by calling the new keyword. So, this tightly couples the `Client` class to the `ShippingService` class. What if tomorrow we need to use the `LoggingShippingService` class instead of `ShippingService`? Also, suppose `ShippingService` talks to the database to calculate the shipping cost, then how will we unit test it? As a unit test should not cross its boundary, we could've used a mock, but our `Client` class is already hardcoded to use the `ShippingService` class. So, what should we do? Let's see how IoC helps us and the modified code looks like this:

```
public class Client {
  // with IoC
  private IShippingService _shippingService;

  Client(IShippingService shippingService) {
    _shippingService = shippingService;
  }

  public ShowShippingCost() {
    Console.WriteLine("The total shipping cost is {0}",
      _shippingService.CalculateShippingCost());
  }
}
```

Here, the `Client` class only specifies that it needs (or has a dependency on) `IShippingService`. It is up to the IoC container to hand over an instance of `ShippingService` whenever some class has a dependency on `IShippingService`. Now, we can specify the dependencies either in configuration (through XML files) or in code as follows:

```
Container.Register<IShippingService, ShippingService>();
```

The preceding line of code tells the IoC container that whenever some class has a dependency on `IShippingService`, hand it an instance of `ShippingService`. This way, for our tests, we can inject a different object for `IShippingService`, as follows:

```
Container.Register<IShippingService, MockShippingService>();
```

Some of the modern IoC frameworks make it even easier by autoregistering the dependencies as long as they follow a convention. Also, in a typical IoC framework, dependencies can be injected into an object using either of the following:

- **The constructor**: This is called the constructor injection
- **A field**: This is called the setter injection
- **The parameters of a method**: This is called the method injection (which is least commonly used)

There's just one more thing to consider — how should the container decide whether it has to always inject a new instance of a dependency or a singleton instance? Well, most of the time, the default is to inject a new instance, but with Angular, the default is a singleton.

 By default, Angular's IoC container only supports a singleton life cycle, so the injected dependency is a singleton.

Dependency injection (or IoC) libraries or frameworks are available for most of the popular object-oriented languages today. With most of them, they have to be downloaded as separate libraries. For example, .NET has Unity (https://msdn. microsoft.com/en-us/library/ff647202.aspx) or Spring.NET (http:// springframework.net/), Java has Guice (https://code.google.com/p/google-guice/), and so on. Angular makes it easy by bundling an in-built dependency injection framework. So, let's see how to do dependency injection in Angular.

We'll take the code introduced in *Chapter 1, AngularJS Rationale and Data Binding*, and modify it a little bit. We'll introduce a service called employeeSvc, which looks like the following lines of code:

```
'use strict';
app.service('employeeSvc', function () {

  var Employee = function (name, age) {
    this.name = name;
    this.age = age;
  };

  Var getEmployees = function () {
    return [
      new Employee("First employee", 56),
      new Employee("Second employee", 44),
      new Employee("Last employee", 32)
    ];
```

```
    };

    // Public API
    this.Employee = Employee;
    this.getEmployees = getEmployees;
});
```

[dependency-injection-ex\employee.svc.js]

We've taken the `Employee` and `getEmployees` function from `EmployeeCtrl` from *Chapter 1, AngularJS Rationale and Data Binding,* and put them into `employeeSvc`. Now, let's inject `employeeSvc` into `EmployeeCtrl` and use the functions from this service as shown in the following code:

```
'use strict';

app.controller('EmployeeCtrl', ['$scope', 'employeeSvc',
  function ($scope, employeeSvc) {

    $scope.employeeData = {
      employees: employeeSvc.getEmployees()
    };
  }
]);
```

[dependency-injection-ex\employee.ctl.js]

If you notice the highlighted code, `EmployeeCtrl` specifies a dependency on `employeeSvc`, and it is Angular's responsibility to hand `EmployeeCtrl` an instance of `employeeSvc`. We are telling Angular about the dependencies by passing the names of dependencies in an array—the `['$scope', 'employeeSvc', ...]` array—this is called **inline array annotation**. We can instead use the following code:

```
'use strict';

app.controller('EmployeeCtrl', function ($scope, employeeSvc) {

    $scope.employeeData = {
      employees: employeeSvc.GetEmployees()
    };
  }
);
```

This code will still work fine. This is called **implicit annotation** as Angular tries to infer the names of dependencies based on the function parameter names, but this is *not* the preferred way. It will give us problems when we minify our code. Since minification leads to name mangling, the names of the function parameters, `$scope` and `employeeSvc`, might get minified to, say, s and e. However, the code still refers to `$scope` and `employeeSvc`, so our code will break.

There is a tool called `ng-annotate` (`https://github.com/olov/ng-annotate`) that can automate the process of adding or removing AngularJS dependency injection annotations. This tool could be run as one of the steps of the build process.

Filters

It often happens that we need to show filtered data. In this case, we can include logic in one of the functions in a service. However, this logic can get lost if a service has many methods. Similarly, we might have to format some data before showing it in the view. Angular introduces filters for precisely these things—either format the value of an expression for display or filter values from an array. Angular comes with some of the most common filters to format number, currency, or date. Refer to the built-in filters available at `https://docs.angularjs.org/api/ng/filter`.

Let's write a custom filter. In our previous example, our service returns some employees. Let's add a few more employees whose age is more than 58 years. Let's assume that the retirement age is 60 years, and anyone whose age is 58 years or more is about to retire. Then, let's filter the employees. So, here's the modified service:

```
'use strict';

app.service('employeeSvc', function () {

  var Employee = function (name, age) {
    this.name = name;
    this.age = age;
  };

var getEmployees = function () {
    return [
      new Employee("First employee", 56),
      new Employee("First old employee", 58),
      new Employee("Second employee", 44),
      new Employee("Second old employee", 59),
      new Employee("Last employee", 32)
    ];
```

```
    };

    // Public API
    this.Employee = Employee;
    this.getEmployees = getEmployees;
});
```

[filter-ex\employee.svc.js]

We've added a few senior employees. So, now, let's write a filter to only show employees who are about to retire:

```
'use strict';

app.filter('seniorEmployeesFltr', function () {
  return function (items) {
    return _.filter(items, function (item) {
returnitem.age >= 58;
    });
  };
});
```

[filter-ex\seniorEmployee.flt.js]

In the preceding code, '_' refers to the excellent Underscore library (http://underscorejs.org/). This library provides many utility functions found in almost all functional programming languages or even in LINQ (from C#), and 'filter' is one of the examples.

 Don't forget to refer to underscore.js in the index.html file.

This is how we use it in the view:

```
<div>
  <h1>Employee data:</h1>
  <h3>In a table (with the filter) -</h3>
  <table>
    <tr>
      <th>Name</th>
      <th>Age</th>
    </tr>
    <tr ng-repeat="employee in employeeData.employees |
      seniorEmployeesFltr">
      <td>{{employee.name}}</td>
```

```
      <td>{{employee.age}}</td>
    </tr>
  </table>

  <br />
  <h3>In a list (without the filter) -</h3>
  <ul>
    <li ng-repeat="employee in employeeData.employees">
      Employee number {{$index}} is - {{employee.name}} -
        {{employee.age}} years old
    </li>
  </ul>
</div>
```

```
[filter-ex\employee.tpl.html]
```

The syntax to apply filters to expressions is as follows:

```
{{ expression | filter }}
```

Filters can be chained and can also have arguments. Visit `https://docs.angularjs.org/guide/filter` for further information about filters. With filters under our belt, let's look at another important feature that Angular provides: that is the feature of communicating with our backend APIs by making AJAX requests.

Promise

While working with Angular/JavaScript, or any technology for that matter, there are scenarios when we need to make asynchronous calls—a very common example is of calling a web API. Obviously, when we call a remote API, we can't call it synchronously, because all further processing stops until that call completes. One of the ways of calling a function asynchronously is using a callback. However, callbacks make the code look convoluted. Sometimes, if you have deeply nested callbacks, then life becomes even more difficult. Promises solve these issues and make the intent of the code very clear. The Promise API is part of the ECMAScript 6 (ES6 Harmony) proposal, but there are implementations of it, which we can use even now.

A Promise object (`https://developer.mozilla.org/en-US/docs/Web/JavaScript/Reference/Global_Objects/Promise`) is used for deferred and asynchronous computations. A Promise object is in one of the following states:

- **Pending**: This is an initial state, not fulfilled or rejected
- **Fulfilled**: This indicates successful operation

- **Rejected**: This indicates rejected operation
- **Settled**: This indicates that Promise is either fulfilled or rejected, but not pending

The idea that makes a Promise intuitive is that it lets an asynchronous method call return a value (just like a synchronous call). However, instead of returning the final value, the asynchronous method returns a promise of having a value at some point in the future. A `Promise` object looks like this:

```
new Promise(function(resolve, reject) { ... });
```

The first argument (resolve) fulfills the Promise, while the second argument (reject) rejects it. The most important method of a `Promise` object is the *then* method. This method gets called when either the pending promise has been fulfilled with a value or rejected with a reason.

The $q service

The `$q` service of Angular is modelled on the lines of ES6 promises, though not all of the supporting methods from ES6 Harmony promises are available yet. Check out the documentation of the `$q` service for more details at `https://docs.angularjs.org/api/ng/service/$q`.

The $http service

The `$http` service is a core Angular service. This service is used to communicate with remote HTTP servers via the browser's `XMLHttpRequest` object or JSONP. The `$http` API is based on the promise APIs exposed by the `$q` service. This service, unsurprisingly, exposes methods that reflect the HTTP verb names, `get`, `head`, `post`, `put`, `delete`, and so on. The typical way of calling these methods is as follows:

```
$http.get('/someUrl')
    .success(function(data, status, headers, config) {
      // this callback is called asynchronously
      // when the response is available
    })
    .error(function (data, status, headers, config) {
      // called asynchronously if an error occurs
      // or server returns response with an error status
    });
```

So, let's see an example of using the $http service. Postcodes.io is a free and open source postcode and Geolocation API for the UK. It exposes many API endpoints. We'll specifically use the one that gives us information about a random postcode, and the API endpoint is http://api.postcodes.io/random/postcodes. If you try clicking on this link, you'll see some information about a random postcode from the UK. So, here's the important piece of code:

```
'use strict';

app.service('postCodeSvc', ['$http', function ($http) {

var getRandomPostCode = function (success, error) {

    $http.get('http://api.postcodes.io/random/postcodes')
      .success(function(data, status, headers, config) {
        success(data, status, headers, config);
      })
      .error(function(data, status, headers, config) {
        error(data, status, headers, config);
      });
  };

    this.getRandomPostCode = getRandomPostCode;
}]);
```

[ajax-ex\postcode.svc.js]

Notice that we inject the $http service in our postCodeSvc service. Then, we define a getRandomPostCode method, which internally calls the $http.get method. This method accepts a success callback as the first parameter and an error callback as the second parameter. This is because the call to the $http service will either succeed or fail. If the http.get method succeeds, then the success callback is called; otherwise, the error callback is called. In these two callbacks, we call the respective callbacks passed to our getRandomPostCode method.

Let's look at the controller now:

```
'use strict';

app.controller('PostCodeCtrl', ['$scope', 'postCodeSvc',
  function ($scope, postCodeSvc) {

    $scope.postCodeData = {};

var success = function (data, status, headers, config) {
```

```
        $scope.postCodeData.result = data.result;
          };

    var error = function (data, status, headers, config) {
        $scope.postCodeData.error = data;
          };

        // call this function which will get the
        // data asynchronously
        postCodeSvc.getRandomPostCode(success, error);
      }
    ]);
```

[ajax-ex\ postcode.ctl.js]

We define the success and error functions to be passed as callbacks to the getRandomPostCode method of the postCodeSvc service. Again, we need these callbacks because the http.get method is called asynchronously, and one of these callbacks is called when this method completes. In the successful case, we set the result property of the postCodeData object on $scope. In the case of an error, we set the error property. Then, the view just displays the information returned by the API:

```
    <div>
      <h1>Postcode info:</h1>
      Postcode: {{postCodeData.result.postcode}} <p />
      Country: {{postCodeData.result.country}} <p />
      Longitude: {{postCodeData.result.longitude}} <p />
      Latitude: {{postCodeData.result.latitude}} <p />
    </div>
```

[ajax-ex\ postcode.tpl.html]

Similarly, we can call other methods of the $http service. Refer to https://docs.angularjs.org/api/ng/service/$http for more information about the $http service.

The $resource service

When we have to deal with a RESTful API, $http proves to be rather low level. We might have to write a lot of boilerplate code to call the methods exposed by the API. This is where the $resource service comes in handy. It returns a resource object that has convenience methods that map to their HTTP verbs' counterparts. So, for example, the get method of the $resource service maps to the HTTP 'GET' method, the save method maps to POST, and the remove and delete methods map to DELETE. The query method maps to GET but has the isArray property set to true. This means it maps to a method that returns all the records (similar to get all).

Node.js and Express-based API sample

For this demo, I've written a small Node.js backend application that exposes a REST API for our Employee object used earlier. For simplicity, it just holds the data in memory and is for illustration purposes only. If you have an API ready, then you can skip this part and directly jump to the next section (which describes how to use the $resource service).

This section assumes that you have Node.js (http://nodejs.org/) and Yeoman (http://yeoman.io/) installed. I've generated the skeleton of this application using the Yo-based AngularJS fullstack generator (https://github.com/DaftMonk/generator-angular-fullstack). The discussion of the Node.js or Express part of this application is beyond the scope of this book. However, the main code is contained in [resource-ex\server\main.js], which contains the various routes for the application, and [resource-ex\server\routes\index.js], which contains methods that map to these routes.

A better $http service

So, let's see why $resource is a higher level abstraction than the $http service. Let's look at the following service:

```
'use strict';

app.service('employeeSvc', ['$resource',
  function ($resource) {
var baseApiPath = 'http://localhost\\:9002/api/';
var employeeApiPath = baseApiPath + 'employees/:id';

    var Employee = $resource(employeeApiPath, {
'update': {
  method: 'PUT'
```

```
        }
    });

    return {
        Employee: Employee
    };
  }
]);
```

[resource-ex\app\scripts\employee.svc.js]

We inject the `$resource` service in `employeeSvc`. Our `employee` resource is available at `/api/employees`, so you may guess the various RESTful methods and the corresponding URLs. Finally, we return the `Employee` resource. Also, note that by default, the `update` method is not exposed by the `$resource` service. Hence, we return it along with the `$resource` service and map it to the HTTP PUT method. We can also customize the behavior of this service by passing in a hash of custom actions. For example, if we set cache to `true`, the `$http` cache is used to cache the GET request. Now, let's see how we can call this resource from `MainCtrl`:

```
'use strict';

app.controller('MainCtrl', ['$scope', 'employeeSvc',
  function ($scope, employeeSvc) {

    var Employee = employeeSvc.Employee;
    var employees = Employee.query();
    var employee = Employee.get({ id: 1 });

    $scope.employeeData = {
      employees: employees,
      employee: employee
    };
  }
]);
```

[resource-ex\app\scripts\controllers\main.js]

The `employeeSvc` service is injected in `MainCtrl`, and we store the `Employee` resource in a variable with a similar name. From there on, we can easily call the various RESTful methods on our resource; two examples, `query` and `get`, are shown in the preceding code. Calling other methods is equally easy.

Summary

In this chapter, we learned about dependency injection and why it is needed. Then, we looked into Angular's support for dependency injection. After that, we saw how to format/filter data using filters, and learned how to write custom filters. Then, we learned about promises and saw how the $http service implements promises-based APIs. Finally, we looked at how the $resource service is a higher level abstraction over the $http service and how it makes calling RESTful services a breeze. Next, we'll learn how to make the UI more declarative using Angular directives.

3
Custom Controls

So far, in our study of Angular, we've seen concepts (such as MVC, dependency injection, and so on) which are available in other programming languages or frameworks and you would be right in thinking, how this sets Angular apart from many other frameworks. With our current knowledge and understanding of Angular, we can write perfectly functional and beautiful-looking applications, but it still doesn't make our frontend code more maintainable—for sure, we've structured our JavaScript code into services or filters, which are injected into controllers (which might live in one or more modules), but think hard, there is still a core piece of frontend code which hasn't seen any improvement. That core piece is the HTML part.

In this chapter, we will cover the following topics:

- What are directives and why do we need them
- Naming convention of directives
- How to write directives
- Different types of directives
- Isolate scopes
- Transclusion
- Directives which communicate

Directives

The HTML code (without the directives) is still made up of `divs` after `divs` nested inside one another, and those `divs` make no semantic sense; except for the various `class` attribute values that you attach to them (or however else you have tried to give them meaning). But wouldn't it be nice if you could instead, structure your HTML like this:

```
<employee id="1"></employee>
```

Or maybe like this:

```
<address type="corporate"></address>
```

Then, you get a nice little piece of UI which displays the full address or information of the employee.

So what are directives? To repeat an oft-quoted cliché, directives teach old HTML some new tricks, and they are the ones which help us in writing custom controls. So we should write directives when we want to refactor repeated (HTML) code, to create new HTML markup and when we need to manipulate the DOM directly.

As per Angular, it is an anti-pattern to manipulate the DOM in your controllers. You must use directives for any kind of DOM manipulation.

We can write directives to represent custom HTML attributes, elements, comments, or to represent custom CSS classes — the default being attributes and elements.

Defining a directive

A directive must be registered with a module by calling the directive function. This function takes the normalized name of the directive and a factory function which returns a **Directive Definition Object (DDO)** as follows:

```
angular.module('app', []).directive('myDirective', function() {
    return myDDO;
});
```

Here, myDirective is the name of the directive and myDDO is the directive definition object. A DDO is an object whose fields tell the compiler what the directive does. The main fields of the DDO are as follows:

```
{
  restrict: 'AEC', // specifies if this directive is an element,
attribute or class
  template: '', // a string used to generate mark-up
  templateUrl: '', // if template is not provided inline, then the URL
where the template will be found
  scope: false, true or {}, // whether to create a new child scope or
to create an isolated scope
  transclude: true, // whether to extract the contents of the element
where the directive appears and make it available to the directive
  controller: fn, // a function that acts as a controller for this
directive
  compile: fn, // a function that can manipulate the source DOM
  link: fn // a function that links the directive to scope
}
```

For more details on the DDO, please refer to: `https://docs.angularjs.org/api/ng/service/$compile#directive-definition-object`.

Directive compilation phases

When Angular compiles a template, it tries to match each element, attribute, comment, and CSS class against the list of registered directives. Whenever it matches a directive, Angular calls the directive's compile function, which returns a linking function.

The compilation phase is done before the scope has been prepared, so no scope data is available to the compile function.

Once all the directives are compiled, Angular creates the scope and starts linking those directives with the scope using the `link` function.

At the linking phase, the scope attached to the directive, and the linking function sets up bindings between the DOM and the scope.

Normalization

Angular normalizes the name of an element or attribute to figure out which elements match which directive. Directives are looked up based on their camelCase case-sensitive names, for example, `myDirective`. However, since HTML is case insensitive, we refer to this directive in our HTML elements in one of the following ways:

`my-directive`, `my_directive`, or `my:directive`

We can further prefix these names with either `data-` or `x-`.

The best practice is to use the dash-delimited format, for example, `my-directive`.

Directive types

Using directives, we can create custom elements, attributes, comments, or classes by setting an appropriate value of the `restrict` key of the DDO. The different restrict options which we can set are as follows:

- `'A'`: This only matches the attribute name
- `'E'`: This only matches the element name
- `'C'`: This only matches the class name

These options can all be combined as needed, so `'AEC'` matches either the attribute, the element, or the class name.

Directive scopes

If a directive has to do something meaningful, it needs a scope object. We can supply a scope to a directive in three different ways, to be specified in the DDO:

- `scope: false`: This means reuse the outer scope from the place where the directive is included. This is the default.

- `scope: true`: This means create a child scope which prototypically inherits from the scope where the directive is included.

- `scope: {}`: This means create an isolated scope for the directive which is totally isolated from the outer (or parent) scope.

Writing directives

Now that we've talked a lot about theory, let's put it into practice and write some directives. We'll start with very simple examples and go on to build complex ones, highlighting various aspects involved in writing directives. We'll keep using employee-related data which we've used in earlier examples to keep things simple, so here's our first simple directive.

Custom attributes

This directive uses an inline template and inherits the scope from the controller. This is not a good practice and is for illustration purposes only (as this is our very first directive). Here's the controller:

```
app.controller('EmployeeCtrl', ['$scope',
  function ($scope) {

    var Employee = function (name, age) {
      this.name = name;
      this.age = age;
    };

    var GetEmployees = function () {
      return [
        new Employee("First employee", 56),
        new Employee("Second employee", 44),
        new Employee("Last employee", 32)
      ];
    };

    $scope.employeeData = {
```

```
      employees: GetEmployees()
    };
  }
]);
```

[Chapter3\directive-ex\employee.ctl.js]

Here's the directive:

```
app.directive("myEmployee", function () {
  return {
    template: 'Name - {{employeeData.employees[0].name}}, Age -
    {{employeeData.employees[0].age}}'
  };
});
```

[Chapter3\directive-ex\employee.dir.js]

Remember we talked about the Directive Definition Object (DDO), so here the directive returns an object with only the `template` value set. So, in this case, our function returns an HTML template which shows an employee's information. Please note that the directive has inherited the scope from the controller (which is putting a list of employees in the scope), and so has access to the `employeeData` object.

Now let's look at the HTML code:

```
<div>
  <h1>Employee data:</h1>
  <div my-employee></div>
</div>
```

[Chapter3\directive-ex\employee.tpl.html]

Isn't it simple? We've now started to abstract away HTML code just like we've been doing it for our JavaScript code (or code in any other object-oriented language). The `my-employee` attribute in the preceding HTML code refers to our `myEmployee` directive defined in the previous code (as per the naming conventions described earlier). In this example, we are only showing the name and age of the employee, but we could have shown a lot more data regarding an employee, and the resulting HTML (where the directive is being used) would still be the same. The only thing that would change is the code (or template, in this case) in the directive. The directive that we just saw, is an example of a 'template expanding' directive.

Another example of such a directive is showing an address in the UI. An address typically consists of a house number, street number, city, state, and zip, and we would have to repeat this fragment of HTML in different screens where the address is to be shown. Also, if the way this information is displayed has to be changed, it has to be changed in many places, and so, a directive is a perfect way to abstract away this piece of code. So now, even our HTML code follows the don't repeat yourself (DRY) principle. You must obviously be thinking that writing HTML templates inside of the directive (as we've shown in our earlier example) is ugly. You are right, and this is where the `templateUrl` option comes into the picture. Here's the same example using the `templateUrl` option. For simplicity, I've renamed the view-related template to `employee-view.tpl.html`. With these changes, our directive code looks like this:

```
app.directive("myEmployee", function () {
  return {
    templateUrl: 'employee.tpl.html'
  };
});
```

[Chapter3\template-url-ex\employee.dir.js]

Our employee template for the directive is:

```
<h5>Name-</h5>
{{employeeData.employees[0].name}}

<h5>Age-</h5>
{{employeeData.employees[0].age}}
```

[Chapter3\template-url-ex\employee.tpl.html]

Hopefully, you are now realizing the power of Angular directives. But there's a lot more, so let's continue digging.

The directives which we've written so far have to be specified as HTML attributes. However, that is just one way of writing directives, so let's convert one of our existing directives to be written as an element.

Custom elements

Here, we'll use the `restrict` option of the DDO to specify that our directive should be used as an HTML element (by setting its value to E). Here's the relevant code:

```
app.directive("myEmployee", function () {
  return {
    restrict: 'E',
```

```
        templateUrl: 'employee.tpl.html'
    };
});
```

[Chapter3\custom-element-ex\employee.dir.js]

Here's the changed HTML (for the view):

```
<div>
  <h1>Employee data (without using a directive):</h1>
  <label for="name">Name</label>
  <input id="name" ng-model="employeeData.first.name" />

  <h5>Age-</h5>
  {{employeeData.first.age}}

  <h1>Employee data (from a directive):</h1>
  <my-employee></my-employee>
</div>
```

[Chapter3\custom-element-ex\employee-view.tpl.html]

The template for the directive remains the same:

```
<h5>Name-</h5>
{{employeeData.first.name}}

<h5>Age-</h5>
{{employeeData.first.age}}
```

[Chapter3\custom-element-ex\employee.tpl.html]

Notice that we are showing the same data twice—once without using a directive (with a label and an input tag), whereas the second view of the same data comes from a directive. We've done this to show you an important point. Currently, the input element is bound to employeeData.first.name and the directive template also makes use of the same data. So what do you think happens if you change the name in the input element? Yes, the corresponding name coming from the directive template also gets changed, which makes it abundantly clear that the directive is inheriting the scope from the parent (which is the controller). This is OK for demonstration purposes but is not a good option when we want to create reusable components, because we don't want anyone to mess with the scope of our directive, and that's where isolate scope comes into the picture (which is discussed in the next section).

So how do you decide between a custom element and a custom attribute? Use an element when you are creating a component and you know what data to display (in the component). This way you can create a **Domain Specific Language** (DSL) for the user interface elements of your application. Use an attribute when you are enhancing the functionality of an existing element.

Isolate scopes

As we've mentioned earlier, it's not very useful to let the directive use the outside scope. Because then, the directive is always coupled with the controller. So what we should do is map the outer scope to the directive's inner scope, and we do this by creating what is called an **isolate scope**. The way we do it is by setting the scope option of the DDO.

The scope object contains a property for each isolate scope binding. There are three ways in which we can supply data to our isolate scope from the attributes: data bind (=), interpolate (@) and expression (&). For example:

```
scope: {
    key1: '=attr1',
    key2: '@attr2',
    key3: '&attr3'
}
```

Here, we are creating an isolate scope binding with three properties named key1, key2, and key3. These properties respectively, get the values from the three different attributes, as specified by =attr1, @attr2, and &attr3.

The attributes in the scope are normalized like directive names, so if the attribute name is my-attr (as in `<div my-attr="value">`), you'd specify a binding to myAttr.

There is a shorter syntax for achieving the same effect. When the name of the attribute is the same as the name that we want to give in the isolate scope, we can simply write the following:

```
scope: {
    employee: '='
}
```

The =attr option in the scope

We'll modify the earlier example just a little bit to illustrate the usage of an isolate scope. So here's the modified code:

```
<div>
  <h1 style="color:forestgreen">Employee data (without using a
directive):</h1>
  <label for="name">Name</label>
  <input id="name" ng-model="employeeData.first.name" />

  <h5>Age-</h5>
  {{employeeData.first.age}}

  <h1 style="color:red">Employee data (from a directive):</h1>
  <my-employee info="employeeData.second"></my-employee>

  <h1 style="color:blueviolet">Back from the directive</h1>
  {{employeeData.second.name}}
</div>
```

[Chapter3\isolate-scope-ex\employee-view.tpl.html]

Note that we are passing the data of the second employee to our directive through the info attribute. Here's the changed directive code:

```
app.directive("myEmployee", function () {
  return {
    restrict: 'E',
    scope: {
      employee: '=info'
    },
    templateUrl: 'employee.tpl.html'
  };
});
```

[Chapter3\isolate-scope-ex\employee.dir.js]

In this, we are creating an isolate scope for the directive using the scope property where we are specifying the value of the employee property to be equal to the value passed to the info attribute from the view (in the preceding code snippet).

Now, let's look at the following directive template code:

```
<h3>Trying to access the parent scope</h3>
<h5>Name-</h5>
{{employeeData.first.name}}

<h5>Age-</h5>
{{employeeData.first.age}}

<hr>

<h3>From the isolate scope</h3>
<h5>Name-</h5>
<input id="name" ng-model="employee.name" />

<h5>Age-</h5>
{{employee.age}}
```

[Chapter3\isolate-scope-ex\employee.tpl.html]

You'll realize, after looking at the directive template, that although from this template we are trying to display information for two employees, one using the parent scope, using {{employeeData.first.name}} and then using the employee property on the directive's scope, using ng-model="employee.name", the data doesn't get displayed using the parent scope. This proves that the two scopes are now different and the directive has access only to its isolate scope.

One thing which might *not* be so apparent from the preceding code is the data which we are displaying in the view under the Back from the directive heading—if you change the name of the employee (which is being displayed by the directive's isolate scope), the name of the employee changes under the Back from the directive heading as well, which means that the second employee's data is being shared by the view and the directive scopes.

So the =attr scope option allows us to set a bidirectional, two-way binding between data in the controller's and the directive's scopes.

The @attr option in the scope

The @ isolate scope lets us read the value of an attribute. Let's look at an example; the controller is very simple:

```
app.controller('EmployeeCtrl', ['$scope',
    function ($scope) {
        $scope.person = {
```

```
        firstName: 'Bruce',
        lastName: 'Lee'
    };
  }
]);
```

[Chapter3\at-scope-ex\employee.ctl.js]

The directive is simple, too:

```
app.directive("myEmployee", function () {
  return {
    scope: {
      firstName: '@',
      lastName: '@'
    },
    templateUrl: 'employee.tpl.html'
  };
});
```

[Chapter3\at-scope-ex\employee.dir.js]

Here, firstName and lastName are attributes whose value is being set to @.
Here's the view:

```
<div my-employee first-name="{{person}}" last-name="{{person.
lastName}}"></div>
```

[Chapter3\at-scope-ex\employee-view.tpl.html]

The view sets the value of the firstName attribute to {{person}} and the lastName
attribute to {{person.lastName}}. Here's the directive template:

```
<div>First name is {{firstName}}</div><br>
<div>Last name is {{lastName}}</div>
```

[Chapter3\at-scope-ex\employee.tpl.html]

The directive can now directly access the values of the firstName and lastName
isolate scope properties. However, when you look at the view, you'll see the following:

First name is {"firstName":"Bruce","lastName":"Lee"}

Last name is Lee

So as you can see, Angular has interpolated the value of the person object to a string,
as seen in the view for First name. The last name is correctly displayed because we
are passing the person.lastName string value.

So, interpolation (using @attr) converts an object to a string, and then we cannot access any properties of the object.

The &attr option in the scope

We've seen how we bind data using the =attr and interpolate data using @attr scope options in the previous examples. Now we'll discuss the &attr scope option in the following example. The &attr option lets us create a callback from the directive. Here's a part of the controller:

```
$scope.buttonClick = function (message) {
        alert(message);
}
```

[Chapter3\and-scope-ex\employee.ctl.js]

Here's the directive:

```
app.directive("myEmployee", function () {
  return {
    restrict: 'E',
    scope : {
      'click': '&onClick'
    },
    templateUrl: 'employee.tpl.html'
  };
});
```

[Chapter3\and-scope-ex\employee.dir.js]

Notice that the directive has an isolate scope property of click whose value is &onClick. Hence we pass this value from the view:

```
<my-employee on-click="buttonClick(message)">
</my-employee>
```

[Chapter3\and-scope-ex\employee-view.tpl.html]

The directive provides the value of the message as follows:

```
This text and the button comes from the directive.
<input type="button" ng-click="click({message: 'This msg comes from
the directive'})" value="Click me!" />
```

[Chapter3\and-scope-ex\employee.tpl.html]

So, as you can see, we use the &attr option when we want the directive to expose an API to the view (or the outside world) for binding to behaviors.

Now, we could have used the `buttonClick` function of the view directly from the directive without setting up an isolate scope, but that would've tightly coupled the directive to the view, and whenever the function name is changed in the view (for any reason), we'll have to make the corresponding change in the directive. But now, the view can call the function by any name, and it just has to pass the correct name of the function to the directive using the `on-click` attribute (or whatever mechanism that you set up).

Transclusion

Sometimes, we'll need to create directives that might wrap arbitrary content. In such cases, instead of passing in a string or an object to the directive, we would want to pass an entire template (of HTML). So, let's see how to achieve that. The controller is similar to the earlier examples and is demonstrated in the following code:

```
app.controller('EmployeeCtrl', ['$scope',
  function ($scope) {

    var Employee = function (name, age) {
      this.name = name;
      this.age = age;
    };

    var GetEmployees = function () {
      return [
        new Employee("First employee", 56),
        new Employee("Second employee", 44),
        new Employee("Last employee", 32)
      ];
    };

    var employees = GetEmployees();

    $scope.employeeData = {
      first: employees[0],
      second: employees[1]
    };
  }
]);
```

[Chapter3\transclude-ex\employee.ctl.js]

Let's see the view code:

```
<my-employee info="employeeData.second">
  However, this content comes from the view.
  <h5>Name-</h5>
  {{employeeData.first.name}}
  <h5>Age-</h5>
  {{employeeData.first.age}}
</my-employee>
```

[Chapter3\transclude-ex\employee-view.tpl.html]

Note that we are wrapping arbitrary content inside the my-employee directive. By arbitrary, we mean you could include any other valid HTML content and it would still work. Here's the directive code:

```
app.directive("myEmployee", function () {
  return {
    restrict: 'E',
    transclude: true,
    scope: {
      employee: '=info'
    },
    templateUrl: 'employee.tpl.html'
  };
});
```

[Chapter3\transclude-ex\employee.dir.js]

First, we are specifying transclude: true which allows the directive to wrap any content inside it and finally the directive template as follows:

```
This content comes from the directive.
<h3>Name-</h3>
{{employee.name}}
<h3>Age-</h3>
{{employee.age}}
<p></p>

<div style="border: 1px solid black;">
    <div style="background-color: beige" ng-transclude></div>
</div>
```

[Chapter3\transclude-ex\employee.tpl.html]

We put an `ng-transclude` directive from wherever we want the view content to be visible inside the directive. In this case, the view content is available inside the `div` element with the beige color background, and it is pretty easy to figure out which content comes from the directive and which comes from the view.

So, isolate scopes give directives the ability to encapsulate data and its behavior so that the directives remain unaffected by the changes outside.

Custom classes

Writing custom classes or comment directives is similar to writing custom attributes or elements. However, it is preferable to use directives via tag names (elements) and attributes.

Directives that manipulate the DOM

We can create a directive which manipulates the DOM. Such a directive uses the link option which takes a function with the following three parameters:

- `scope`: This is the Angular scope object
- `element`: This is the (jqLite wrapped) element that this directive matches
- `attrs`: These are the attributes which are passed to this directive

So, let's see an example of such a directive. The controller is pretty simple:

```
app.controller('EmployeeCtrl', ['$scope',
  function ($scope) {
    $scope.firstName = "Bruce";
  }
]);
```

[Chapter3\dom-ex\employee.ctl.js]

The controller exposes a `firstName` property on the `$scope` object. The view sets the value of the `lastname` attribute of the directive to the value `Lee` as shown in the following code:

```
<div my-employee lastname="Lee"></div>
```

[Chapter3\dom-ex\employee-view.tpl.html]

The directive uses the `link` function as follows:

```
app.directive("myEmployee", function () {
  return {
    link: function (scope, element, attrs) {
      var name = scope.firstName + ' ' + attrs.lastname;
      element.text(name);
      $(element).effect('shake');
    }
  };
});
```

[Chapter3\dom-ex\employee.dir.js]

The signature of the `link` function is as described in the preceding code. Notice that inside the `link` function we can access the `firstName` property on the controller's `$scope` object using the function's first (`scope`) parameter as `scope.firstName`. We can access the value of the `lastname` attribute using the third (`attrs`) parameter and we can access the element using the second (`element`) parameter of the `link` function. The `text` function on the element is available because it is a jQuery wrapped element as we are including jQuery before Angular in our HTML page:

```
<script src="https://cdnjs.cloudflare.com/ajax/libs/jquery/
  2.1.3/jquery.js"></script>
<script src="https://cdnjs.cloudflare.com/ajax/libs/jqueryui/
  1.11.2/jquery-ui.js"></script>
```

[Chapter3\dom-ex\index.html]

If we hadn't referred to jQuery in the previous code, then the element would've been a jqLite wrapped element. So, in the directive, we just combine the first and the last name, assign it to the element, and use the jQuery UI's (https://jqueryui.com/) shake effect (https://api.jqueryui.com/shake-effect/) to shake the element. So, preferably do your DOM manipulations in a directive as shown in the preceding code.

Communication between directives

What if we want to build a component that is composed of many directives? In such cases, it might be necessary that those directives have a way to talk to each other. To do so, a child (contained) directive can set the value of the `require` property of the DDO to one of the parent (container) directives as follows:

```
scope: {
    require: '^parentDirective'
}
```

The ^ prefix means that this directive searches for the controller on its parents. So, if the specified controller is not found, then `$compile` throws an error. Without the ^ prefix, the search for the controller is done only on the directive element. We can also make the controller optional by putting ? as a prefix for the directive name, for example:

```
scope: {
    require: '?parentDirective'
}
```

If the directive is not provided, then the fourth parameter to the link function (which is the directive controller, as shown in the following code snippet) is null.

So, let's see an example:

```
<my-employee name="Employee 1">
  Employee 1
  <addresses>
    Addresses
    <address type="home">Address 1</address>
    <address type="office">Address 2</address>
  </addresses>
</my-employee>
```

[Chapter3\dir-comm-ex\employee-view.tpl.html]

As you'll notice, `my-employee`, `addresses`, and `address` are all directives. Here are the directives:

```
app.directive("myEmployee", function () {
  return {
    restrict: 'E',
    scope: {
      name: '@'
    },
    transclude: true,
    controller: function ($scope) {
      this.getName = function () {
        return $scope.name;
      };
    },
    template: '<div ng-transclude style="background-
      color:blueviolet">{{name}}</div>'
  };
});
app.directive("addresses", function () {
```

```
      return {
        restrict: 'E',
        scope: {},
        transclude: true,
        template: '<div ng-transclude style="background-
          color:pink"></div>'
      };
    });
    app.directive("address", function () {
      return {
        require: '^myEmployee',
        restrict: 'E',
        scope: {
          type: '@'
        },
        transclude: true,
        link: function (scope, element, attrs, myEmployeeCtrl) {
          console.log(myEmployeeCtrl.getName() + ' ' + scope.type);
        },
        template: '<div ng-transclude style="background-
          color:powderblue"></div>'
      };
    });
```

[Chapter3\dir-comm-ex\employee.dir.js]

Notice that each of the directive sets transclude to true so that the content inside can be included. Additionally, the myEmployee directive declares a controller using the controller function and declares a getName function returns name , which is on the directive's scope. Now the address directive has a require option set to ^myEmployee – which means it looks for the controller on any of the parents of the directive. And finally, the employee directive uses a link function whose fourth parameter is the myEmployee controller, which we have named here as myEmployeeCtrl (this could be named anything else). So now the myEmployeeCtrl parameter can be used inside of the address directive. You must be thinking what are the differences between a controller and a link function? Well, the differences are listed as follows:

- Just like any other controller, dependencies can be injected into directive controllers.

- All directive controllers have $scope injected into them. Apart from this, other services such as $timeout or $rootScope can be injected as well.

- Additionally, three special services can be injected into directive controllers: `$element`, `$attrs`, and `$transclude`.

- Finally, as mentioned previously, a directive controller exposes an API, whereas a `link` function can interact with controllers using `require`.

In case a directive wants to use controllers of multiple directives, then the `require` option can accept an array as follows:

```
require: ['^myEmployee', '^myOtherDirective']
```

Also, the fourth parameter of the `link` function is an array of controllers as follows:

```
link: function (scope, element, attrs, controllers)
```

These are in the same order as mentioned by the `require` option, and we can get the individual controllers from this array.

You can also refer to the excellent Angular documentation on directives: *Directives developer guide* (`https://docs.angularjs.org/guide/directive`).

Summary

In this chapter, we learned all about directives and how directives enable us to drastically transform our HTML code by helping us write custom elements, attributes, classes, and comments. If carefully designed, directives help us write the DSL for our frontend code. We also talked about isolating the directive scope and including content in the directive using the `transclude` option. Finally, we talked about how directives can communicate with each other.

In the next chapter, we'll learn about Firebase, its benefits, and why to use it. We'll also learn about AngularFire, which is the officially supported Angular binding for Firebase.

4
Firebase

We can write web applications by using the frameworks of our choice—be it server-side MVC frameworks, client-side MVC frameworks, or some combination of these. We can also use a persistence store (a database) of our choice—be it an RDBMS or a more modern NoSQL store. However, making our applications real time (meaning, if you are viewing a page and data related to that page gets updated, then the page should be updated or at least you should get a notification to refresh the page) is not a trivial task and we have to start thinking about push notifications and what not. This does not happen with Firebase.

In this chapter, we will cover the following topics:

- A brief description about various types of persistence mechanisms
- A brief comparison of local versus hosted databases
- What Firebase is, why to use it, and different use cases where Firebase can be useful
- How to use Firebase
- How to structure data while using Firebase
- Why denormalizing data can be good sometimes
- What is AngularFire?

Persistence

One of the very early decisions a developer or a team has to make when building any production-quality application is the choice of a persistent storage mechanism. Until a few years ago, this choice, more often than not, boiled down to a relational database such as Oracle, SQL Server, or PostgreSQL. However, the rise of NoSQL solutions such as MongoDB (http://www.mongodb.org/) and CouchDB (http://couchdb.apache.org/) – document-oriented databases or Redis (http://redis.io/), Riak (http://basho.com/riak/), keyvalue stores, Neo4j (http://www.neo4j.org/), and a graph database – has widened the choice for us. Please check the Wikipedia page on NoSQL (http://en.wikipedia.org/wiki/NoSQL) solutions for a detailed list of various NoSQL solutions including their classification and performance characteristics.

There is one more buzzword that everyone must have already heard of, **Cloud**, the short form for **cloud computing**. Cloud computing briefly means that shared resources (or software) are provided to consumers on a paid/free basis over a network (typically, the Internet). So, we now have the luxury of choosing our preferred RDBMS or NoSQL database as a hosted solution. Consequently, we have one more choice to make – whether to install the database locally (on our own machine or inside the corporate network) or use a hosted solution (in the cloud).

As with everything else, there are pros and cons to each of the approaches. The pros of a local database are fast access and one-time buying cost (if it's not an open source database), and the cons include the initial setup time. If you have to evaluate some another database, then you'll have to install the other database as well. The pros of a hosted solution are ease of use and minimal initial setup time, and the cons are the need for a reliable Internet connection, cost (again, if it's not a free option), and so on.

Considering the preceding pros and cons, it's a safe bet to use a hosted solution when you are still evaluating different databases and only decide later between a local or a hosted solution, when you've finally zeroed in on your database of choice.

What is Firebase?

So, where does Firebase fit into all of this? Firebase is a NoSQL database that stores data as simple JSON documents. We can, therefore, compare it to other document-oriented databases such as CouchDB (which also stores data as JSON) or MongoDB (which stores data in the BSON, which stands for binary JSON, format).

Although Firebase is a database with a RESTful API, it's also a real-time database, which means that the data is synchronized between different clients and with the backend server almost instantaneously. This implies that if the underlying data is changed by one of the clients, it gets streamed in real time to every connected client; hence, all the other clients automatically get updates with the newest set of data (without anyone having to refresh these clients manually).

So, to summarize, Firebase is an *API* and a *cloud service* that gives us a *real-time and scalable* (NoSQL) backend. It has libraries for most server-side languages/frameworks such as Node.js, Java, Python, PHP, Ruby, and Clojure. It has official libraries for Node.js and Java and unofficial third-party libraries for Python, Ruby, and PHP. It also has libraries for most of the leading client-side frameworks such as AngularJS, Backbone, Ember, React, and mobile platforms such as iOS and Android.

Firebase – benefits and why to use?

Firebase offers us the following benefits:

- It is a cloud service (a hosted solution), so there isn't any setup involved.
- Data is stored as native JSON, so what you store is what you see (on the frontend, fetched through a REST API) – WYSIWYS.
- Data is safe because Firebase requires 2048-bit SSL encryption for all data transfers.
- Data is replicated and backed-up to multiple secure locations, so there are minimal chances of data loss.
- When data changes, apps update instantly across devices.
- Our apps can work offline – as soon as we get connectivity, the data is synchronized instantly.
- Firebase gives us lightning fast data synchronization. So, combined with AngularJS, it gives us *three-way data binding* between HTML, JavaScript, and our backend (data).

With two-way data binding, whenever our (JavaScript) model changes, the view (HTML) updates itself and vice versa. But, with three-way data binding, even when the data in our database changes, our JavaScript model gets updated, and consequently, the view gets updated as well.

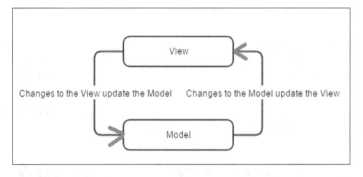

- Last but not the least, it has libraries for the most popular server-side languages/frameworks (such as Node.js, Ruby, Java, and Python) as well as the popular client-side frameworks (such as Backbone, Ember, and React), including AngularJS. The Firebase binding for AngularJS is called AngularFire (https://www.firebase.com/docs/web/libraries/angular/).

Firebase use cases

Now that you've read how Firebase makes it easy to write applications that update in real time (and you'll see that in action in the next chapter on AngularFire), you might still be wondering what kinds of applications are most suited for use with Firebase. Because, as often happens in the enterprise world, either you are not at liberty to choose all the components of your stack or you might have an existing application and you just have to add some new features to it. So, let's study the three main scenarios where Firebase can be a good fit for your needs.

Apps with Firebase as the only backend

This scenario is feasible if:

- You are writing a brand-new application or rewriting an existing one from scratch
- You don't have to integrate with legacy systems or other third-party services
- Your app doesn't need to do heavy data processing or it doesn't have complex user authentication requirements

In such scenarios, Firebase is the only backend store you'll need and all dynamic content and user data can be stored and retrieved from it.

Existing apps with some features powered by Firebase

This scenario is feasible if you already have a site and want to add some real-time capabilities to it without touching other parts of the system. For example, you have a working website and just want to add chat capabilities, or maybe, you want to add a comment feed that updates in real time or you have to show some real-time notifications to your users.

In this case, the clients can connect to your existing server (for existing features) and they can connect to Firebase for the newly added real-time capabilities. So, you can use Firebase together with the existing server.

Both client and server code powered by Firebase

In some use cases, there might be computationally intensive code that can't be run on the client. In situations like these, Firebase can act as an intermediary between the server and your clients. So, the server talks to the clients by manipulating data in Firebase. The server can connect to Firebase using either the Node.js library (for Node.js-based server-side applications) or through the REST API (for other server-side languages). Similarly, the server can listen to the data changes made by the clients and can respond appropriately. For example, the client can place tasks in a queue that the server will process later. One or more servers can then pick these tasks from the queue and do the required processing (as per their availability) and then place the results back in Firebase so that the clients can read them.

Firebase is the API for your product

You might not have realized by now (but you will once you see some examples) that as soon as we start saving data in Firebase, the REST API keeps building side-by-side for free because of the way data is stored as a JSON tree and is associated on different URLs. Think for a moment if you had a relational database as your persistence store; you would then need to specially write REST APIs (which are obviously preferable to old RPC-style web services) by using the framework available for your programming language to let external teams or customers get access to data. Then, if you wanted to support different platforms, you would need to provide libraries for all those platforms whereas Firebase already provides real-time SDKs for JavaScript, Objective-C, and Java.

So, Firebase is not just a real-time persistence store, but it doubles up as an API layer too.

Getting started with Firebase

Getting started with Firebase is pretty easy—first, we have to sign up for a free account. Once we do that, a new Firebase is created for us with a unique URL ending in `firebaseio.com`. We'll use this URL to store and sync data in Firebase.

Installing Firebase

There are two ways of using Firebase: One is to reference the JavaScript client library directly from the Firebase CDNs:

```
<script src="https://cdn.firebase.com/js/client/2.1.1/
  firebase.js"></script>
```

The other is to use bower (`http://bower.io/`), which is a package manager for the web, if we want to install Firebase as a local dependency. Please check *Appendix A, Yeoman* on how to use bower:

```
bower install firebase
```

A nice thing about Firebase is that the Firebase API for Node.js is exactly the same as the Firebase JavaScript API, which means that it can be used in the same way on the client and the server side.

Once you create a new Firebase account and log in to it, you'll see a dashboard with the ability to create a new app as shown in the following screenshot:

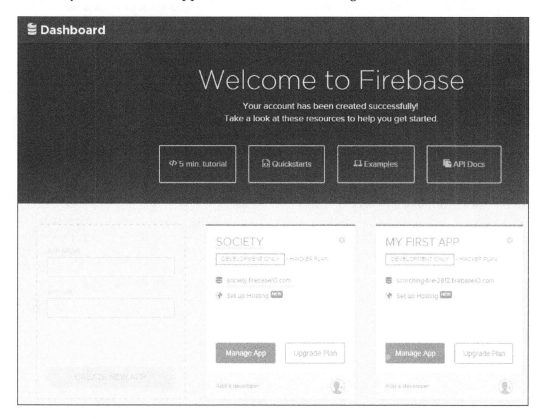

Please note that you can create a new app (the button underlined in yellow). By creating a new app, we are in fact creating a new URL where all our data relating to this app will be stored. So, as you can see in the preceding screenshot, I created a new app called **SOCIETY** and Firebase created a `society.firebaseIO.com` URL for us. We'll be using this app (or URL) for storing data related to our society application, which we are going to build (using AngularFire) in the next chapter.

Structuring data

Every application involves data, so for talking about how to structure data, let's choose a simple problem domain. I'll assume that you are staying in an apartment, and this apartment is part of a bigger apartment complex. The management of the complex has to maintain a lot of information about the complex, such as how many buildings there are in the complex, how many apartments there are in each building, and who the owners and tenants of these apartments are. Then, it has to keep track of the number of vehicles that each owner/tenant has. Keeping this problem space in mind, let's see how we can store and fetch data from Firebase.

Since Firebase is a NoSQL store, which doesn't have SQL-like querying capabilities, we need to pay upfront attention to the structure of data, how the data will be read back later, and how to make this process of reading as easy as possible. NoSQL stores operate on one underlying principle, which is—disk space is cheap, but the user's time is not, which essentially means that duplicating some data to make reads faster is fine, but then special care needs to be taken while writing data because we might have to write it in more than one place.

Considering the preceding mentioned problem domain, first, let's look at a naïve way of structuring our data:

```
{
  "buildings": {
    "building1": {
      "number": "1",
      "name": "First Building",

      "apartments": {
        "apartment1": { "number": "101",
          "residents": {
            "resident1": { "name": "John Doe" },
            "resident2": { "name": "Jane Doe" }
          }
        }
      }
    },
    ...
  }
}
```

Since Firebase allows us to nest data up to 32 levels deep, we are tempted to structure our data in a nested, tree-like fashion. However, when we fetch data for a node in Firebase, we also fetch its children. So, it's better to keep things as flat as possible. With the preceding nested design, even if we have to show the names (or numbers) of all the buildings, we have to download the entire buildings tree to the client.

Nesting data is not a recommended practice in Firebase.

Our second attempt at structuring the data might be to replicate an SQL-like structure as shown in the following code:

```
{
  "buildings": {
    "building1": {
      "number": "1",
      "name": "First Building"
    },
    "building2": {
      "number": "2",
      "name": "Second Building"
    }
  },
  "apartments": {
    "apartment1": {
      "number": "101",
      "belongsTo": "building1"
    },
    "apartment2": {
      "number": "102",
      "belongsTo": "building1"
    }
  },
  "residents": {
    "resident1": {
      "name": "John Doe",
      "livesIn": "apartment1"
    },
    "resident2": {
      "name": "Jane Doe",
      "livesIn": "apartment2"
    }
  }
}
```

But, what if we need to show all the residents of a particular apartment? In SQL, every resident would have a reference to the apartment he was living in, so you could use **where apartment = apartmentId** but Firebase doesn't have the **where** query. As per the current structure, we could retrieve a resident only if we knew its resident ID, which we do not.

Denormalizing data

So, what should we do? In our case, to enable retrieving the list of residents for an apartment, we'll explicitly store that list with each apartment. This is called denormalization of data, which means splitting the data into separate paths so that it can be efficiently downloaded in segments, as it is needed. Have a look at this flattened structure:

```
{
  "apartments": {
    "apartment1": {
      "number": "101",

      // an apartment's residents are stored here
      "residents": {
        // the value 'true' doesn't matter here
        // what matters is that the key exists
        "resident1": true
      }
    },
    "apartment2": { ... },
  }
}
```

The same structure applies to the buildings and apartments relation:

```
{
  "buildings": {
    "building1": {
      "number": "1",
      "name": "First Building"

      // a building's apartments are stored here
      "apartments": {
        // the value 'true' doesn't matter here
        // what matters is that the key exists
        "apartment1": true,
        "apartment2": true
```

```
        }
    },
    "building2": { ... }
    }
}
```

We are duplicating some data, but this is the key to writing scalable applications. Usually, reads are more common than writes, so this is an acceptable trade-off, with the added price that we'll have to take much more care while updating/deleting data. Consider what happens when we have to delete a resident—not only do we have to delete the individual resident, but we also have to delete the link of this resident from the apartment he was living in. Similarly, if we are adding a new resident, then we again have to add the link to this resident in the appropriate apartment. So, before you start writing any Firebase application, please spend some time upfront to figure out how you are going to structure data because while doing this exercise, you'll be forced to think what queries your app will need.

AngularFire

AngularFire is the officially supported AngularJS binding for Firebase. Although we could use the Firebase JavaScript SDK to interact with Firebase, AngularFire abstracts a lot of complexities involved in synchronizing data, and only in advanced cases, we'll need to drop down to the Firebase JavaScript SDK. We'll examine AngularFire in *Chapter 5, Getting Started with AngularFire*.

Summary

In this chapter, we talked about different types of persistence mechanisms, for example, RDBMS and NoSql (document, key-value, and graph) stores, and also looked at Firebase. Then, we talked about the benefits Firebase has to offer and saw different use cases where Firebase can be used. We also read about AngularFire, which is the officially supported Angular binding for Firebase.

In the next chapter, we'll see how to use AngularFire in our Angular applications.

5

Getting Started with AngularFire

As mentioned in the previous chapter on Firebase, AngularFire is the officially supported AngularJS binding for Firebase. Let's get started with AngularFire because that's the library which will primarily be used in our Angular applications to connect to Firebase. One thing to keep in mind is that AngularFire is *not* a wrapper over the *entire* Firebase API, but it makes the job of AngularJS developers very easy, and we'll need to drop down to the Firebase JavaScript SDK only in advanced cases.

In this chapter, we will cover the following topics:

- How to use AngularFire
- Synchronized objects and arrays in AngularFire
- Three-way data binding
- Various authentication options provided by Firebase

AngularFire

When we talk of building any system, we either have to deal with objects, or with collections. Those objects often contain collections, for example, in a one-to-many relationship. So, AngularFire gives us two different services—`$firebaseObject` and `$firebaseArray`—to synchronize objects and arrays with the backend. Let's see how to use each of these services in the following examples.

Synchronized arrays with $firebaseArray()

So, here's our `index.html` file (just the relevant part of the code is shown):

```
<script src="https://cdn.firebase.com/js/client/2.2.3/firebase.js">
</script>
<script src="https://cdn.firebase.com/libs/angularfire/1.0.0/
  angularfire.min.js">
</script>
<script src="https://cdnjs.cloudflare.com/ajax/libs/underscore.js/
  1.7.0/underscore-min.js">
</script>
```

(`Chapter5\sync-objs-arrays\index.html`)

We are referring to `firebase`, `angularfire`, and the Underscore (`http://underscorejs.org/`) libraries from the CDNs. In a real-life scenario, we would have installed them in our application using `'bower'` and referred to these libraries from their local paths.

Here's the main module of the application:

```
var app = angular.module('firebaseApp', [
  'ngRoute',
  'firebase'
]);

// this is the Firebase URL we'll be talking to
// in case of your Firebase account, please modify
// the below URL appropriately
app.constant('FIREBASE_URI', 'https://society.firebaseio.com/');

app.config(function ($routeProvider) {
  $routeProvider
    .when('/', {
      templateUrl: 'main.html'
    })
    .when('/arrays', {
      templateUrl: 'sync-array/syncarray.tpl.html',
      controller: 'SyncArrayCtrl'
    })
    .when('/objects', {
      templateUrl: 'sync-object/object.tpl.html',
      controller: 'SyncObjectCtrl'
    })
    .when('/properties', {
```

```
      templateUrl: 'property/property.tpl.html',
      controller: 'PropertyCtrl'
    })
    .otherwise({
      redirectTo: '/'
    });
  });
```

(Chapter5\sync-objs-arrays\app.js)

First we add the 'firebase' module as a dependency for our firebaseApp Angular app. This gives us access to the $firebaseObject and $firebaseArray service. We can specify these as a dependency in our controllers, services, or factories. Then we register a 'constant' service on our app which contains the Firebase URL where we'll be storing our data. Notice that the URL https://society.firebaseIO.com is the same one that Firebase gave us when we created our Society Firebase app (in the previous chapter). Then we just configure various routes and the corresponding templates and controllers. Let's look at the controller now:

```
app.controller('SyncArrayCtrl', ['$scope', 'syncArraySvc',
  function ($scope, syncArraySvc) {

    $scope.building = new Building();

    $scope.buildings = syncArraySvc.getBuildings();

    $scope.addBuilding = function () {
      syncArraySvc.addBuilding(angular.copy($scope.building));
      $scope.building = new Building();
    };

    $scope.updateBuilding = function (id) {
      syncArraySvc.updateBuilding(id);
    };

    $scope.removeBuilding = function (id) {
      syncArraySvc.removeBuilding(id);
    };
  }
]);
```

(Chapter5\sync-objs-arrays\sync-array\syncarray.ctl.js)

The SyncArrayCtrl controller is exposing a variable on $scope called building, which is an instance of a Building domain object. This is being bound to the textboxes where the user can enter information for a new Building. The controller also exposes another variable on $scope called buildings, which is used to display the existing buildings. The controller also has a dependency on syncArraySvc, and various controller methods (such as addBuilding or updateBuilding) are just delegating to the corresponding service methods. This is one of the best practices in Angular:

> *Try to keep your controllers thin and delegate as much responsibility to the services/factories as you can.*

The view is pretty simple. There is one form to create a new building:

```
<form>
<div class="form-group">
<label for="number">Building Number</label>
<input type="number" class="form-control" id="number" ng-
   model="building.buildingNumber" placeholder="Enter building
   number">
</div>
<div class="form-group">
<label for="name">Building Name</label>
<input type="text" class="form-control" id="name" ng-
   model="building.buildingName" placeholder="Enter building name">
</div>
<button type="submit" class="btn btn-primary" ng-
   click="addBuilding()">Submit</button>
</form>
```

(Chapter5\sync-objs-arrays\sync-array\syncarray.tpl.html)

The building number and name textboxes are bound to the building. buildingNumber and building.buildingName properties, respectively, and the Submit button is bound to the addBuilding method. The remaining part of the form displays the existing buildings where you can modify or delete any existing building:

```
<tr ng-repeat="(id, building) in buildings">
<form class="form-inline">
<td><input type="number" class="form-control" ng-
   model="building.buildingNumber"></td>
<td><input type="text" class="form-control" ng-
   model="building.buildingName"></td>
<td>
<button type="button" class="btn btn-default" ng-
   click="updateBuilding(id)">
<span class="glyphicon glyphicon-edit"></span>
```

```
    </button>
    </td>
    <td>
    <button type="button" class="btn btn-default" ng-
      click="removeBuilding(id)">
    <span class="glyphicon glyphicon-trash"></span>
    </button>
    </td>
    </form>
    </tr>
```

(Chapter5\sync-objs-arrays\sync-array\syncarray.tpl.html)

 The preceding two snippets are part of the same file.

The bindings of the textboxes are similar to what was just explained. Only the edit and delete button icons are bound to the updateBuilding and removeBuilding methods by passing in the ID of the particular record. There's one new construct in the previous snippet related to ng-repeat:

ng-repeat="(id, building) in buildings"

This is just a variation of the ngRepeat directive (which we've seen before), where id is the index of the element in the collection over which we are iterating. This is the id which is being passed to the updateBuilding and removeBuilding methods.

Let's look at the most important part of this application, which is the service:

```
app.factory('syncArraySvc', ['FIREBASE_URI', '$firebaseArray',
    function (FIREBASE_URI, $firebaseArray) {
      var buildingsUri = FIREBASE_URI + '/buildings';
      var ref = new Firebase(buildingsUri);
      var buildings = $firebaseArray(ref);

      var getBuildings = function () {
        return buildings;
      };

      var addBuilding = function (item) {
        buildings.$add(item);
      };

      var updateBuilding = function (id) {
        buildings.$save(id);
```

```
    };

    var removeBuilding = function (id) {
      buildings.$remove(id);
    };

    return {
      getBuildings: getBuildings,
      addBuilding: addBuilding,
      updateBuilding: updateBuilding,
      removeBuilding: removeBuilding
    }
  }]);
```

(Chapter5\sync-objs-arrays\sync-array\building.svc.js)

Our `syncArraySvc` service has a dependency on the `$firebaseArray` service and the `FIREBASE_URI` constant service defined along with the module earlier. The `$firebaseArray` service is used for synchronizing Firebase data with Angular apps. It contains some helper methods for writing data to Firebase, as well as for reading data into synchronized collections. The `$firebaseArray` service takes one argument: A Firebase reference. So we create a Firebase reference by passing in the URL where we'll be storing the data. For storing the data related to buildings, we append `/buildings` to `FIREBASE_URI`.

The `$firebaseArray` service returns the data stored on a particular URL as a collection. This collection is a synchronized array, meaning that the array is kept in sync with the remote changes. The collection returned by this method is a read-only collection, so we should *not* use regular JavaScript array methods such as `push`, `pop`, or `splice` to modify the structure of the array. Instead, special methods such as `$add`, `$save`, and `$remove` are provided, which are being used inside our service methods `addBuilding`, `updateBuilding`, and `removeBuilding`, respectively.

There's just one small piece of code remaining and that is the `building` domain model:

```
    var Building = function(number, name) {
      this.buildingNumber = number;
      this.buildingName = name;
    };
```

(Chapter5\sync-objs-arrays\domain\building.js)

Currently, this domain model is just a bunch of setters, but, in real life, the domain model class should be *rich*; meaning it should contain *business rules* (related to the particular model) and it might also contain validation logic to make sure that any instance of this model should be valid.

Real-time applications

You might not have realized by now that we have a running application which syncs data in real time for every connected client. Run the application, click on the **Synchronized Arrays** button, and add a few buildings. Now, either open another instance of the same browser, or maybe a different browser, and navigate to the same application (URL). Maximize the first instance of the browser and resize the second browser to a size smaller than the first one so that the first one is visible (in the background). Now try adding, modifying, or deleting a few buildings and you'll notice that the browser window in the back (the bigger one) reflects the changes you make almost instantaneously, without you having to refresh the first browser or implementing any kind of PUSH notifications. This is the power of synchronized arrays, that is, all the connected clients get updates in real time.

Once we've entered data for a few buildings, we can view it in the Firebase dashboard:

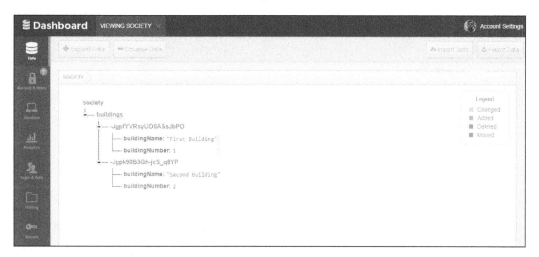

You can see the data under the `buildings` node that is under the root `society` node. So the entire data is getting stored as a JSON tree. Notice that there are buttons to import and export data in the top-right corner of the dashboard.

Firebase also gives us Vulcan, which is a Chrome DevTools extension which lets us inspect and edit data from within Chrome. Once you install the extension, it looks like this:

Synchronized objects with $firebaseObject()

Typically, an object is composed of key-value pairs and is used when we want to store data for an individual record. The code for synchronized objects is very similar to the preceding code and is contained in the `Chapter5\sync-objs-arrays\sync-object` folder. However, let's see some interesting code in action that shows the various properties and functions of synchronized objects and arrays.

When you run the application, you'll see a **Properties** button and when you click on it, the following template file is rendered (The following snippet is just a part of the template file):

```html
<br>
<div class="panel panel-info" ng-if="doesDataExist()">
<div class="panel-heading">
<h3 class="panel-title">Properties / Functions of synchronized
objects</h3>
</div>
<div class="panel-body">
    Properties
<ul class="list-inline">
<li ng-repeat="key in objectkeys">{{key}}</li>
</ul>
    Functions
<ul class="list-inline">
<li ng-repeat="function in objectfunctions">{{function}}</li>
</ul>
</div>
</div>

<br>

<div class="panel panel-info" ng-if="doesDataExist()">
<div class="panel-heading">
<h3 class="panel-title">Properties / Functions of synchronized
arrays</h3>
</div>
<div class="panel-body">
    Properties
<ul class="list-inline">
<li ng-repeat="key in arraykeys">{{key}}</li>
</ul>
    Functions
<ul class="list-inline">
<li ng-repeat="function in arrayfunctions">{{function}}</li>
</ul>
</div>
</div>
```

(Chapter5\sync-objs-arrays\property\property.tpl.html)

The ng-if directive removes or recreates a portion of the DOM based on the value of the expression/function provided to it. So here, it'll either create, or remove the two divs where we show the properties and functions associated with the synchronized objects or arrays. The various ng-repeat directives iterate over different properties and functions of synchronized objects and arrays. Here's the controller:

```
app.controller('PropertyCtrl', ['$scope', 'propertySvc',
    function ($scope, propertySvc) {

        $scope.syncArray = propertySvc.getSyncArray();

        $scope.doesDataExist = function () {
            return $scope.syncArray.length > 0;
        };

        $scope.showPropertiesAndFunctions = function () {
            $scope.arraykeys = _.keys($scope.syncArray);
            $scope.arrayfunctions = _.functions($scope.syncArray);

            var building =
                propertySvc.getSyncObject($scope.syncArray[0].$id);
            building.$loaded()
                .then(function (item) {
                    $scope.objectkeys = _.keys(item);
                    $scope.objectfunctions = _.functions(item);
                })
                .catch(function(error) {
                    console.log("Error:", error);
                });
        };
    }
]);
```

(Chapter5\sync-objs-arrays\property.ctl.js)

The doesDataExist function returns true if some data is found at the buildings child of our main URL location. The interesting piece of code is in the showPropertiesAndFunctions function. It uses the keys and functions functions of the Underscore library, which return all the names of the synchronized object's/array's properties and a sorted list of names of every method in that object/array, respectively. This function also uses the $loaded function on the building synchronized object (which is returned by the service). The $loaded function returns a promise which is resolved when the object has been downloaded from Firebase. The service is pretty straightforward:

```
app.factory('propertySvc', ['FIREBASE_URI', '$firebaseArray',
  '$firebaseObject',
  function (FIREBASE_URI, $firebaseArray, $firebaseObject) {
    var buildingsUri = FIREBASE_URI + '/buildings';
    var ref = new Firebase(buildingsUri);
    var buildings = $firebaseArray(ref);

    var getSyncArray = function () {
      return buildings;
    };

    var getSyncObject = function (id) {
      return $firebaseObject(ref.child(id));
    };

    return {
      getSyncArray: getSyncArray,
      getSyncObject: getSyncObject
    }
}]);
```

(Chapter5\sync-objs-arrays\property.svc.js)

The `getSyncArray` function returns a synchronized array, whereas the `getSyncObject` function returns a synchronized object. The running application looks like this:

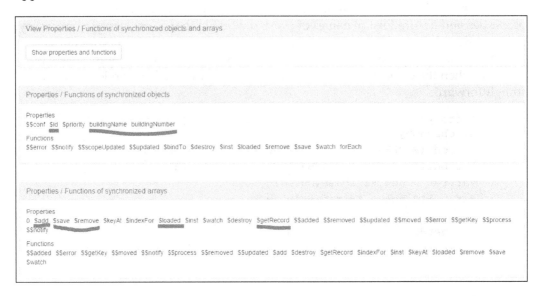

Some of the functions and/or properties that we've used in our previous example have been highlighted in the preceding screenshot. Please check the AngularFire API documentation (`https://www.firebase.com/docs/web/libraries/angular/api.html`) for more details about the AngularFire API and the *AngularFire Development Guide* (`https://www.firebase.com/docs/web/libraries/angular/guide.html`) for more conceptual details.

Three-way data binding

You've seen how easy and cool synchronizing the changes from the server is. However, AngularFire takes it a notch further by introducing three-way data binding, whereby it is able to detect local changes, so we don't even have to call `$save()`. We just have to call `$bindTo()` on a synchronized object and any changes in the DOM are pushed to Angular and finally to Firebase. Conversely, any changes to the data get pushed to Angular and finally to the DOM.

So let's see it in action. The code for this example is very similar to the one we used in the synchronized arrays example, with a few changes. Here's the modified `app.js` file:

```
app.config(function ($routeProvider) {
  $routeProvider
```

```
      .when('/', {
        templateUrl: 'main.html'
      })
      .when('/buildings', {
        templateUrl: 'building/buildings.tpl.html',
        controller: 'BuildingsCtrl'
      })
      .when('/buildings/:buildingIndex', {
        templateUrl: 'building/building.tpl.html',
        controller: 'BuildingCtrl'
      })
      .otherwise({
        redirectTo: '/'
      });
  });
```

(Chapter5\three-way-binding\app.js)

Notice here how we are configuring the second route with
/buildings/:buildingIndex. :buildingIndex is the variable part of
the URL. The following code is part of the template file which constructs
this variable URL:

```
<tr ng-repeat="(id, building) in buildings">
<td>
<a href="#/buildings/{{id}}">{{building.buildingNumber}}</a>
</td>
<td>{{building.buildingName}}</td>
</tr>
```

(Chapter5\three-way-binding\building\buildings.tpl.html)

When showing the buildings using ng-repeat, we pass {{id}} to href to construct
the dynamic URL. The service is pretty straightforward:

```
app.factory("buildingSvc", ['FIREBASE_URI', '$firebaseArray',
  '$firebaseObject',
  function(FIREBASE_URI, $firebaseArray, $firebaseObject) {
    var buildingsUri = FIREBASE_URI + '/buildings';
    var buildingsRef = new Firebase(buildingsUri);
    var buildings = $firebaseArray(buildingsRef);

    var getBuildings = function () {
      return buildings;
    };

    var getBuilding = function (index) {
```

```
        var key = buildings.$keyAt(index);
        var buildingRef = buildingsRef.child(key);
        return $firebaseObject(buildingRef);
      };

    return {
      getBuildings: getBuildings,
      getBuilding: getBuilding
    }
  }]);
```

(Chapter5\three-way-binding\building\buildings.svc.js)

The only interesting part is the getBuilding function, which takes a building index, gets its key, and creates a Firebase reference for the relative path of that particular building by calling the child function and passing in the key. Then we create a synchronized object for that building using $firebaseObject. BuildingsCtrl is very straightforward, so here's the maybe more interesting BuildingCtrl:

```
app.controller('BuildingCtrl', ['$scope', '$routeParams',
  'buildingSvc',
  function ($scope, $routeParams, buildingSvc) {

    var hasAnError = false;

    $scope.hasError = function () {
      return hasAnError;
    };

    if ($routeParams.buildingIndex !== null) {
      var index = parseInt($routeParams.buildingIndex);

      if (!isNaN(index)) {
        // create a three-way binding to our building as $scope.
building
        buildingSvc.getBuilding(index).$bindTo($scope,
          "building");
      }
      else {
        hasAnError = true;
      }
    }
  }
]);
```

(Chapter5\three-way-binding\building\building.ctl.js)

The `$routeParams` service is injected in the controller. It allows us to retrieve the current set of route parameters. Since we had specified `:buildingIndex` as a route parameter (while setting up our routes), we retrieve it using `$routeParams.buildingIndex`. The `buildingSvc` service is also injected and the index (of the building) is passed to this service, which returns a synchronized object to us. Finally, we bind the returned synchronized object to `$scope` using the `$bindTo` method. The first argument to this method is `$scope` and the second is the name of the variable which we want to appear on `$scope`. Since the value of the second argument here is `building`, `$scope.building` is available to the view(s):

```html
<div class="panel panel-default">
<div class="panel-heading">
<h3 class="panel-title">Update building</h3>
</div>
<div class="panel-body">
<form>
<div class="form-group">
<label for="number">Building Number</label>
<input type="number" class="form-control" id="number"
  ng-model="building.buildingNumber" placeholder="Enter building
  number">
</div>
<div class="form-group">
<label for="name">Building Name</label>
<input type="text" class="form-control" id="name"
  ng-model="building.buildingName" placeholder="Enter building name">
</div>
</form>
</div>
</div>
```

(Chapter5\three-way-binding\building\buildings.tpl.html)

When you click on any of the building number links on the existing buildings page, you'll see the data for that building reflected in the two input textboxes on the update building page. Also, notice that there is no `Submit` button for this form and we are not even calling `$save()` anywhere. Now these textboxes are bound directly to Firebase and sync their changes with Firebase automatically. So, if you make any changes to the data, that data will automatically be saved to Firebase.

> Although three-way data bindings are extremely convenient, we should be careful while using these with deeply-nested data structures. For performance reasons, their use should be limited to synchronizing key-value pairs which don't get changed by too many users.

Authentication

No application can be built without including some kind of authentication/authorization mechanism, and Firebase applications are no exception. Hence, Firebase provides us with many options for authenticating users as follows:

- **Custom**: This is for complete control over authentication. This requires server-side code and by using it we can generate our own login tokens.

- **E-mail and password**: We can register and authenticate users using e-mail and password.

- **Anonymous**: For small one-off tasks, we can use anonymous authentication where users are not required to register with us. A unique identifier is generated for each user that lasts as long as their session.

- **OAuth providers for Facebook, Twitter, Google, and GitHub**: We can authenticate users using any of these OAuth providers.

We have to configure each provider individually and enable it in the Firebase dashboard before any of the clients can use it. Please check *AngularFire Development Guide* (https://www.firebase.com/docs/web/libraries/angular/guide.html) for detailed information about different authentication mechanisms and other information. We'll see an example of one of the authentication mechanisms in our final chapter, Applied Angular and AngularFire.

Summary

In this chapter, we talked about the synchronized objects and arrays provided by AngularFire and how they make it very easy to write real-time applications. Then we saw how three-way data binding takes it even further and how UI elements on screen can be directly synchronized with Firebase. Finally, we talked about the various authentication mechanisms provided by Firebase.

In the next chapter, we'll write a full end-to-end application which will demonstrate all the best practices of Angular and Firebase and will also show authentication in action.

6

Applied Angular and AngularFire

We're finally onto the last chapter of the book and we've barely scratched the surface of AngularFire and Firebase. We haven't looked at any of the authentication mechanisms provided by Firebase. So, let's see that and much more in action.

In this chapter, we will cover the following topics:

- We'll write an example application using the techniques we've learned so far
- We'll also follow some of the best practices to be followed while writing Angular applications
- We'll use the simplest (anonymous) authentication provided by Firebase in our example application
- We'll see the difference between Angular factory and service

Firebase anonymous authentication

Anonymous authentication is the simplest form of authentication that Firebase supports. It generates a unique identifier for each user as long as their session lasts. The advantage of this approach is that the users don't have to share their personal information. We are going to use this technique in our next example application. We'll use the same problem domain that we discussed in *Chapter 4, Firebase*, and improve our code which we wrote in *Chapter 5, Getting Started with AngularFire*, because the earlier example didn't create any directives. We'll be using the recently released AngularFire 1.0.0 library.

The `index.html` page (as usual) refers to various JS libraries, and the following is the only interesting piece of code:

```
<div class="container">
    <div ng-include="'menu/menu.tpl.html'"></div>

    <div ng-view=""></div>

    <div class="footer">
      <p><span class="glyphicon glyphicon-heart"></span> from the
        Yeoman team</p>
    </div>
  </div>
```

(`Chapter6\example-app\index.html`)

As usual, we have `ng-view` where we'll be showing various screens. Notice that we're also including the HTML fragment related to our menu using `ng-include`. Also, notice that the name of the file `menu/menu.tpl.html` is enclosed in single quotes ''. The reason we are keeping the menu in a separate template is because we want to show/hide certain menu items based on whether the user is logged in or not. We'll be delegating this task to its own controller. So, here's the menu template:

```
<div class="header" ng-controller="MenuCtrl as menuCtrl">
    <ul class="nav nav-pills pull-right">
      <li ng-if="menuCtrl.isLoggedIn()"><a ng-
        href="#/buildings">Buildings</a></li>
      <li ng-if="menuCtrl.isLoggedIn()"><a ng-
        href="#/apartments">Apartments</a></li>
      <li><a ng-href="#/factsvc">Factory-Service</a></li>
      <li class="active"><a ng-href="#/">Home</a></li>
    </ul>
    <h3 class="text-muted">Hello AngularFire anonymous
      authentication</h3>
  </div>
```

(`Chapter6\example-app\menu\menu.tpl.html`)

As mentioned previously, we are assigning a `MenuCtrl` function to the menu using `ng-controller="MenuCtrl as menuCtrl"`, where `menuCtrl` is an alias for `MenuCtrl`. We'll see the advantages of assigning an alias to the controller later in the chapter, but please notice that we are accessing the function `isLoggedIn` defined in `MenuCtrl` using its alias `menuCtrl`. Now, the reason to use an alias for the controller might have become obvious to you. The `ng-if="menuCtrl.isLoggedIn()"` function is used for the `<li>` element shown earlier and it adds or removes the DOM element based on whether the user has logged in or not, so if this function returns true (meaning the user has logged in), this menu element appears, otherwise it doesn't. Let's look at the menu controller now:

```
app.controller('MenuCtrl', ['authTokenFactory',
  function (authTokenFactory) {

    this.isLoggedIn = function () {
      return authTokenFactory.isLoggedIn();
    };

    this.errorDuringLoggingIn = function () {
      return authTokenFactory.errorDuringLoggingIn();
    };
  }
]);
```

(`Chapter6\example-app\menu\menu.ctl.js`)

Notice that the `isLoggedIn` and `errorDuringLoggingIn` methods are defined on the `this` object (not on the `$scope` object as we would usually do). This has been possible because we are using an alias for the controller in the template. We are also injecting the `authTokenFactory` function in our controller (which stores the authorization token for the logged in user), and both the controller methods delegate the decision of whether the user is logged in or not to this factory. Let's look at the factory now:

```
app.factory('authTokenFactory', ['authSvc',
  function (authSvc) {

    var authTokenFactory = {};

    authTokenFactory.login = function () {
      authSvc.login().then(function (authData) {
        authTokenFactory.authData = authData;
        console.log('aTF.aD: ' + authTokenFactory.authData);
      }).catch(function (error) {
        authTokenFactory.error = error;
```

```
        });
    };

    authTokenFactory.logout = function () {
      authSvc.logout();
      authTokenFactory.authData = null;
      authTokenFactory.error = null;
    };

    authTokenFactory.isLoggedIn = function () {
        return (typeof authTokenFactory.authData !== 'undefined')
          && authTokenFactory.authData !== null;
    };

    authTokenFactory.errorDuringLoggingIn = function () {
        return (typeof authTokenFactory.error !== 'undefined')
          && authTokenFactory.error !== null;
    };

    return authTokenFactory;
  }]);
```

(Chapter6\example-app\authToken.fctry.js)

We are injecting the `authSvc` service which does the actual work of logging in/out a user (as we'll see in the following code). Inside the factory, we first instantiate an empty object using `var authTokenFactory = {};`, and all the other methods — `login`, `logout`, `isLoggedIn`, and `errorDuringLoggingIn` — are defined on this object. Note that I've named this object `authTokenFactory`, but we could've used any other name and it would still be ok. The important thing to notice in the `login` function is that we are storing the `authData` and `error` values on this same empty object we defined earlier. So once the user logs in, these values will stay there until he logs out and we can use these in other controllers too. Please also check the *Difference between a factory and a service* section to be clear about the difference between the two. Let's look at the main controller now:

```
app.controller('MainCtrl', ['$scope', 'authTokenFactory',
  function ($scope, authTokenFactory) {

    $scope.isLoggedIn = function () {
      return authTokenFactory.isLoggedIn();
    };

    $scope.errorDuringLoggingIn = function () {
      return authTokenFactory.errorDuringLoggingIn();
```

```
        };

        $scope.login = function() {
          authTokenFactory.login();

          $scope.$watch(function () {
            return authTokenFactory.authData;
          }, function () {
            $scope.authData = authTokenFactory.authData;
          });
        };

        $scope.$watch(function () {
            return authTokenFactory.error;
        }, function () {
            $scope.error = authTokenFactory.error;
        });

        $scope.logout = function () {
            authTokenFactory.logout();
            $scope.authData = null;
        };
      }
    ]);
```

(Chapter6\example-app\main\main.ctl.js)

MainCtrl also gets injected with authTokenFactory and the various functions just delegate to the authTokenFactory function. The login function first calls the authTokenFactory.login() function (which actually logs the user in Firebase) and then watches for changes to the authTokenFactory.authData variable. As soon as there is a value in this variable, we put that same data on $scope so that we could display it on the view. The first argument to the $scope.$watch function is an expression which returns the value that we want to watch. Now if there was a variable called title on $scope, then we could've used the following command:

```
$scope.$watch('title', function() { // do something });
```

But in our case, the variable is not on scope but is a value in authTokenFactory. So we have to use another variation of the $watch method, where we use a function as the watch expression, which returns the value to be watched (as shown in the preceding code). Here, whenever the value of authTokenFactory.authData changes, we want to store that value on our $scope variable. We do the same thing when some error happens by watching the changes to the authTokenFactory.error variable.

The `authTokenFactory` function has a dependency on `authSvc` which is where the interesting login-logout stuff happens with AngularFire:

```
app.service('authSvc', ['FIREBASE_URI', '$firebaseAuth',
  function (FIREBASE_URI, $firebaseAuth) {

    var ref = new Firebase(FIREBASE_URI);
    var auth = $firebaseAuth(ref);

    var login = function () {
      return auth.$authAnonymously();
    };

    var logout = function () {
      return auth.$unauth();
    };

    return {
      login: login,
      logout: logout
    }
}]);
```

(Chapter6\example-app\auth.svc.js)

Notice that the `authSvc` function is now a service, which is injected with the AngularFire service named `$firebaseAuth`, which wraps the authentication methods provided by the Firebase library. The `$firebaseAuth` service takes a Firebase reference as its only argument, and this Firebase reference points to the URL of our Firebase instance. The authentication object (`auth`) returned by the preceding service contains several methods for authenticating users, managing authentication state, managing user accounts, and so on. As anonymous authentication is one of the simplest methods we've used it here, and the `$authAnonymously` method authenticates a Firebase client using a new, temporary guest account. This method returns a promise which is resolved or rejected based on the outcome of the authentication attempt. If successful, it returns an object containing the authentication data about the logged-in user. If unsuccessful, it returns an `Error` object. The `login` method of the `authTokenFactory` sets `authTokenFactory.authData` in the case of successful login or `authTokenFactory.error` in case of any errors. Similarly, we call the `$unauth` method on the `auth` object to un-authenticate a Firebase client. We call this method when we want to log out the current user. Please check the AngularFire API (available at `https://www.firebase.com/docs/web/libraries/angular/api.html`) for more details. Now when we run the application, we see the following screen:

Please note that you see only the `Factory-Service` and `Home` menu items on the top-right corner and a **Please click here** link to log in anonymously. When you click on the link, you might get an error like this:

The error message is a very descriptive one and clearly specifies the action that we need to take: `Error: {"code":"AUTHENTICATION_DISABLED","details":"You can enable anonymous authentication from the \"Login & Auth\" tab at https://society.firebaseio.com."}`. So let's do what we are supposed to do by enabling anonymous authentication from the **Login & Auth** tab of our Firebase dashboard, as shown in the following screenshot:

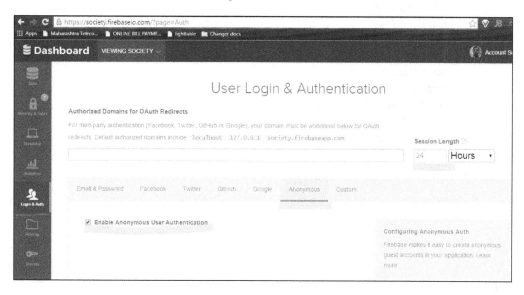

Notice that we can set the length of the session to be anywhere from seconds to hours to months. Once we enable anonymous authentication and try to log in again, we see the following message:

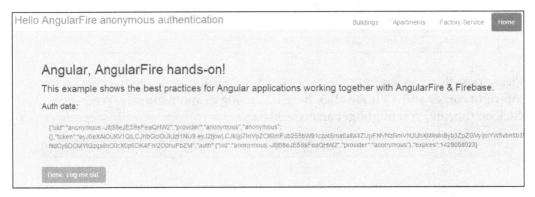

This time the authentication is successful and we see the authentication information for the user like UID, token, expires, and so on. We also see the **Buildings and Apartments** menu items in addition to the previous **Home** option. Let's look at how the routes are defined in the module:

```
app.config(function ($routeProvider) {
  $routeProvider
    .when('/', {
      templateUrl: 'main/main.tpl.html',
      controller: 'MainCtrl as mainCtrl'
    })
    .when('/buildings', {
      templateUrl: 'building/building-view.tpl.html',
      controller: 'BuildingCtrl as buildingCtrl'
    })
    .when('/apartments', {
      templateUrl: 'apartment/apartment.tpl.html',
      controller: 'ApartmentCtrl as apartmentCtrl'
    })
    .when('/factsvc', {
      templateUrl: 'fact-svc/factSvc.tpl.html',
      controller: 'MyCtrl as myCtrl'
    })
    .otherwise({
      redirectTo: '/'
    });
  });
```

(Chapter6\example-app\app.js)

Notice how we are defining various controllers. Each controller is defined along with its alias using the 'controller as' syntax introduced in Angular 1.2.0. The way this syntax works is that it binds the controller to the current $scope. The main advantages of this syntax are given here:

- We don't need to inject $scope into the controllers and whatever properties or methods we want to declare on $scope can be declared on the this object of the controller. Thus we avoid what is commonly derided as the scope soup.

- While referring to any property or method in the DOM, we now have to refer to it using the controller alias making it very obvious as to which property/method belongs to which controller.

So for example, consider the following code (when the controller as syntax is not used when the routes are defined):

```
<div>
{{ name }}
  <div>
    {{ name }}
  </div>
</div>
```

Here we have to figure out from which controller the first {{ name }} is coming and from which controller the second {{ name }} comes (because of the nested scopes). If we use the controller as syntax, the situation becomes very clear:

```
<div>
  {{ employeeCtrl.name }}
  <div>
    {{ departmentCtrl.name }}
  </div>
</div>
```

The whole code is self-explanatory. And the benefit is not limited to when we have nested scopes but it's for precisely every property or method because each of them is accessed via its controller alias. So, it makes life easy when we have to understand/read code written by others (or even by us).

Using the controller as syntax is considered one of the best practices of Angular.

So let's see an example from the application:

```javascript
app.controller('ApartmentCtrl', ['$scope', 'apartmentSvc',
  'buildingSvc',
  function ($scope, apartmentSvc, buildingSvc) {

    var vm = this;
    vm.currentBuilding = null;

    vm.apartment = new Apartment();
    vm.buildings = buildingSvc.findAll();

    vm.insertAndAddReferenceToBuilding = function () {
      apartmentSvc.insertAndAddReferenceToBuilding
        (angular.copy(vm.apartment));
      vm.apartment = new Apartment();
    };

    $scope.$watch(function () {
      return vm.currentBuilding;
    }, function () {
      buildingSvc.setCurrentBuilding(vm.currentBuilding);

      if (vm.currentBuilding) {
        vm.apartments =
          buildingSvc.getApartmentsForCurrentBuilding();
        vm.apartments.$loaded().then(function (data) {
          console.log('apt count: ' + data.length);
        });
      }
    });
  }
]);
```

(Chapter6\example-app\apartment\apartment.ctl.js)

Before you cry foul on seeing $scope injected in the ApartmentCtrl controller, let me explain. First, we capture the this object in the vm variable so that we don't have to deal with these scoping and binding issues. The reason we named it as vm is because the controller actually acts as the view's model (or ViewModel), hence all the properties/methods are declared on this vm instance. If you follow this (or any other) convention, your code becomes more readable and predictable. This advice comes from John Papa's excellent article: *AngularJS's Controller As and the VM Variable* (available at http://www.johnpapa.net/angularjss-controller-as-and-the-vm-variable/). We need to inject $scope into this controller because we want to watch for changes to the currentBuilding variable. You already saw how watches work in the preceding lines. The following code is a part of buildingSvc:

```
app.service('buildingSvc', ['FIREBASE_URI', '$firebaseArray',
    function (FIREBASE_URI, $firebaseArray) {

    var buildingsUri = FIREBASE_URI + 'buildings';
    var buildingsRef = new Firebase(buildingsUri);
    var buildings = $firebaseArray(buildingsRef);

    var currentBuilding = null;

    var getApartmentsForCurrentBuilding = function () {
      var apartmentsRef = buildingsRef.child(currentBuilding +
        '/apartments');
      return $firebaseArray(apartmentsRef);
    };

    var addApartmentForCurrentBuilding = function (apartmentRef) {
      var child = buildingsRef.child(currentBuilding +
        '/apartments/' + apartmentRef.key());
      child.set(true);
    };

    var removeApartmentForCurrentBuilding = function
      (apartmentRef) {
      var child = buildingsRef.child(currentBuilding +
        '/apartments/' + apartmentRef);
      child.remove();
    };
}]);
```

(Chapter6\example-app\building\building.svc.js)

We keep track of all the buildings using $firebaseArray. You have to look at the data to figure out how we maintain the relationships between the data elements, which are buildings and apartments in those buildings in this case:

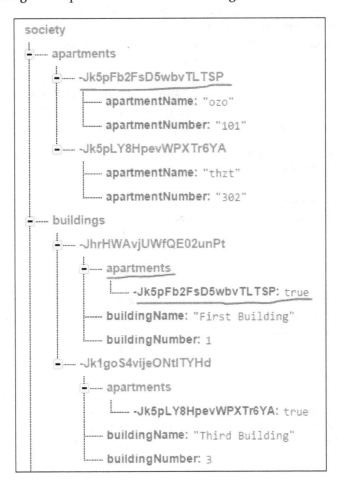

Notice that for **"First Building"**, there is an **apartments** node, where the value of **-Jk5pFb2FsD5wbvTLTSP** key is set to true. Also notice that this is the same key for the apartment number **"101"**.

We are achieving this in the addApartmentForCurrentBuilding function of buildingSvc; we first get to the child of currentBuilding using apartmentRef and then set its value to true (using child.set(true);). We have to use a similar technique to remove the apartment for the current building. This is how relationships are maintained in Firebase (please refer to the Firebase Structuring Data available at https://www.firebase.com/docs/web/guide/structuring-data.html to read more on structuring your data in Firebase). There is some interesting code in the view too (again, a part of the file is shown in the following code snippet):

```html
<br>
<h3>Current Building</h3>
<select class="form-control" ng-
  model="apartmentCtrl.currentBuilding"
        ng-disabled="apartmentCtrl.buildings.length == 0"
        ng-options="building.$id as building.buildingName for
            building in apartmentCtrl.buildings">
  <option value="">Select a building</option>
</select>

<div ng-if="apartmentCtrl.currentBuilding">
  <h3>Apartments</h3>
  <table class="table edit">
    <thead>
    <tr>
      <th>Number</th>
      <th>Name</th>
      <th></th>
    </tr>
    </thead>
    <tbody>
    <tr apartment apartment-ref="{{apartment.$id}}" ng-repeat="(id,
      apartment) in apartmentCtrl.apartments">
      <td><input type="text" ng-
        model="myApartment.apartmentNumber" ng-
        blur="updateItem()"/></td>
      <td><input type="text" ng-model="myApartment.apartmentName"
        ng-blur="updateItem()"/></td>
      <td>
        <a href="#/apartments" ng-click="removeItem()"
          class="navbar-link">Remove</a>
      </td>
    </tr>
    </tbody>
  </table>
</div>
```

(`Chapter6\example-app\apartment\apartment.tpl.html`)

First we use the `ngOptions` attribute to dynamically generate a list of `<option>` elements for the `<select>` element. The syntax of `ngOptions` is like this:

```
ng-options="select as property for item in items"
```

Where item is an individual item in the items' collection, property is the text we want to display in the drop-down box, and select is the value which we want to bind to the value of the `<option>` element. An option element can only be bound to string values at present, so `ngOptions` should be used if the `<select>` model has to be bound to a nonstring value.

Then, while showing apartments for the current building, an apartment directive is used and we pass `apartment.$id` to the apartment-ref attribute. `$id` is the Firebase key where this record is stored (which is like the primary key value). And on `ng-blur`, we call the `updateItem()` method; the blur event fires when the element loses focus, so we are updating the value of the `apartmentNumber` and `apartmentName` properties of an apartment whenever the respective input boxes loses focus. Similarly, we call the `removeItem()` method of the directive when someone clicks the `Remove` link. The directive is pretty straightforward:

```
app.directive('apartment', ['FIREBASE_URI', '$firebaseObject',
'apartmentSvc',
  function (FIREBASE_URI, $firebaseObject, apartmentSvc) {

    var linker = function (scope, element, attrs) {
      scope.apartmentRef = attrs['apartmentRef'];
      scope.myApartment = $firebaseObject(new Firebase(FIREBASE_URI +
        'apartments/' + scope.apartmentRef));
    };

    var controller = function ($scope) {
      $scope.updateItem = function () {
        $scope.myApartment.$save();
      };

      $scope.removeItem = function () {
        apartmentSvc.removeAndRemoveReferenceFromBuilding($scope.
apartmentRef);
      };
    };

    return {
      scope: true,
      link: linker,
```

```
        controller: controller
    };
  }]);
```

(Chapter6\example-app\apartment\apartment.dir.js)

A `$firebaseObject` is injected in the directive and it holds the apartment object, the key of which is being passed by the apartment-ref attribute from the view. This is being stored in the myApartment variable on the isolate scope of the directive, and the `$save` method (of `$firebaseObject`) is called inside updateItem of the directive. For removing an apartment, the removeAndRemoveReferenceFromBuilding method of apartmentSvc is called because not only we have to delete an apartment but also we have to delete the apartment for that particular building. So here's the relevant part of the code for apartmentSvc:

```
app.service('apartmentSvc', ['FIREBASE_URI', '$firebaseArray',
  'buildingSvc',
   function (FIREBASE_URI, $firebaseArray, buildingSvc) {

     var apartmentsUri = FIREBASE_URI + 'apartments';
     var apartmentsRef = new Firebase(apartmentsUri);
     var apartments = $firebaseArray(apartmentsRef);

     var insertAndAddReferenceToBuilding = function (apartment) {
       apartments.$add(apartment).then(function (ref) {
         buildingSvc.addApartmentForCurrentBuilding(ref);
       })
     };

     var removeAndRemoveReferenceFromBuilding = function
       (apartmentRef) {
       var index = apartments.$indexFor(apartmentRef);
       apartments.$remove(index).then(function () {
         console.log('now remove apartment for building: ' +
           apartmentRef);
         buildingSvc.removeApartmentForCurrentBuilding(apartmentRef);
       }, function (error) {
         console.log('Error: ' + error);
       });
     };
  }]);
```

(Chapter6\example-app\apartment\apartment.svc.js)

In the `insertAndAddReferenceToBuilding` function, we call the `$add` method on the apartments `$firebaseArray`, which creates a new apartment. The `$add` method creates a new record in the Firebase and adds the record to our synchronized array. This method returns a promise which is resolved to the Firebase reference (key) for the newly added record (apartment), and this key is used to save the apartment for the current building by calling the `buildingSvc.addApartmentForCurrentBuilding` method. Similarly, we call the `$remove` method on the `$firebaseArray` object to remove the apartment, but before that we have to get the index of the apartment (to remove) using the `$indexFor` method. Once the apartment is removed, we have to remove its reference from the current building using the `buildingSvc.removeApartmentForCurrentBuilding` method.

The rest of the code in the example is easy to comprehend now that you have enough understanding of topics such as AngularJS directives and various Firebase and AngularFire concepts. Check the `createBuilding` and `editBuildings` directives contained in the `Chapter6\example-app\building\create-building.dir.js` and `Chapter6\example-app\building\edit-buildings.dir.js` files respectively to get a taste of how to further encapsulate the UI code in a more DDD fashion.

Difference between a factory and a service

Factories and services are used almost interchangeably in Angular, however there is a subtle but important difference between the two. So let's see their usage and it'll be amply clear when and how to use each one. First let's use the `service` command:

```
app.service('myService', function(){
    this.hello = function() {
        return "Hello World";
    };
});
```

(Chapter6\example-app\fact-svc\my.svc.js)

myService has a single function called hello which returns "Hello World" when called. Now let's use the `factory` command:

```
app.factory('myFactory', function(){
    return {
        hello: function() {
            return "Hello World";
        }
    }
});
```

(Chapter6\example-app\fact-svc\my.fctry.js)

myFactory has a single function called hello which returns "Hello World" when called as well. So what's the difference? For that, let's look at a factory which can accept or maintain some state as shown in the following code:

```
app.factory('myFactoryWithState', function() {
    return function(name) {
        this.name = name;

        this.hello = function() {
            return "Hello " + this.name;
        };
    };
});
```

(Chapter6\example-app\fact-svc\myState.fctry.js)

The myFactoryWithState command also has a single function called hello, but this factory is accepting a name parameter, which can be passed from outside. Now let's see their usage in the controller:

```
app.controller('myCtrl', function(myService, myFactory,
myFactoryWithState) {

    var vm = this;

    var init = function() {
      vm.fromService = myService.hello(); //'Hello World'
      vm.fromFactory = myFactory.hello(); //'Hello World'
      vm.fromFactoryWithData = new
        myFactoryWithState('State').hello(); //'Hello State'
    };

    init();
});
```

(Chapter6\example-app\fact-svc\my.ctl.js)

The two factories defined earlier and the services are injected into myCtrl. The controller is just storing the values returned by various service and factory functions on different scope variables, which are then displayed in the view. But please pay attention to how we instantiated myFactoryWithState; inside the init function, we are using new to instantiate that particular factory, and the factory stores this passed in data in the name variable, so in effect, it can maintain its own state. So, factories offer more flexibility by returning functions which can be called with new keyword.

> *For simplicity, prefer services and when you need to store some data, then use factories.*

The template code is very easy and can be found in the Chapter6\example-app\ fact-svc\factSvc.tpl.html file.

Summary

In this final chapter of the book, you looked at the difference between Angular factory and service. We then built an example using some of the best practices for Angular and used Firebase's anonymous authentication to achieve login/logout from Firebase. We also saw how data is to be structured in Firebase and use it from AngularFire.

A
Yeoman

Today Node.js (available at `http://nodejs.org/`) needs no introduction, but for the benefit of those who haven't crossed paths with it yet, here's an introduction—Node.js lets developers write server-side code in JavaScript. Yes, it's the same JavaScript, which used to run only in browsers until a few years ago. The same JavaScript, which was confined to the frontend, was suddenly unleashed on the world of backend which was previously accessible to server-side languages such as Java, C#, Ruby, Python, and the like.

 Consequently, you can access the filesystem, write data-intensive applications which access relational DBs or NoSQL DBs, write a web server with Node.js, and so on.

Previously, for doing anything with the Web, developers were supposed to learn and write code in at least two different languages—a server-side language and JavaScript. Node.js changed this and made our lives easier because the frontend and the backend code can be written in the same language now.

It is said that for a programming language to gain mass adoption, it needs a successful and famous library/framework. For example, Rails did it for Ruby. Node.js is doing the favors for JavaScript—so much so that this survey (available at `http://adambard.com/blog/top-github-languages-for-2013-so-far/`) pegs JavaScript as the top language for 2013, based on the number of repositories created on GitHub.

Now when we start coding in any language, we typically use an IDE-like Visual Studio for .NET and maybe Eclipse for Java, or we might use powerful text editors such as Sublime Text or Emacs. The extra work these IDEs do for us is to generate a project skeleton when we create a new project. However, the text editors lack this support because they are not programming language-specific. So what do we do when we are starting a new Angular project? Surely, we can create a project structure manually, but it wouldn't be too productive, right? Then we would have to do this cumbersome activity again for any new project we create. Also realize that typically, there are three activities required in a project of reasonable complexity, irrespective of the programming language, where automation could help developers:

- **Scaffolding**: The dictionary meaning of a scaffold is a temporary structure for holding workers and materials during the erection, repair, or decoration of a building. So, scaffolding in programming terms means generating an agreed upon (based on the best practices for that language or framework) folder structure for us.

- **Dependency management**: Any sufficiently complex project has to use external libraries/frameworks, and in this day and age, we can't be expected to manually download the DLLs, JAR files, or JavaScript/CSS files and manually include them in the correct path.

- **Build management**: Once we are done with the development, we need to build the source code and possibly package it as an EXE, JAR file, or a minified JavaScript file.

This is where the tools, which we are going to discuss in the next section, such as NPM or Yeoman come handy.

NPM

Any modern programming language has a package manager for managing external dependencies in your program. In simple terms, it means downloading and using various external libraries/frameworks in your program; for example, Clojure has Leiningen (available at http://leiningen.org/), Ruby has RubyGems (available at https://rubygems.org/), and .NET has Nuget (available at https://www.nuget.org/). NPM (available at https://www.npmjs.com/) is the official package manager for Node.js. NPM is bundled with Node.js these days, so as soon as you install Node.js (for your OS), NPM is ready to serve you.

You might think that you are just developing an Angular application and you don't plan on writing server-side JavaScript (or using Node.js), so why do you even need NPM? The answer to your quandary is that NPM is required to install the other tools mentioned in the next sections, and it's needless to say that you'll thank yourself for installing Node.js and NPM.

Yeoman

As far as I remember, I came across the term scaffolding (available at http://en.wikipedia.org/wiki/Scaffold_(programming)) while reading about Ruby on Rails framework. Scaffolding generates the boilerplate code for us, thereby reducing the grunt work we have to do. For example, it might generate a controller, some views, and the database table based on a model; or it might generate an agreed upon (based on the best practices for that language or framework) folder structure for us at the start of a project.

Yeoman (available at http://yeoman.io/) is a scaffolding tool for writing modern web applications. It is available as an NPM package, so you can install it globally (for a machine) using NPM as follows:

```
npm install -g yo
```

The Yeoman workflow comprises of three tools (which help us automate the three required tasks as discussed previously):

- **yo**: This tool scaffolds out a new application
- **grunt or gulp**: These are the build tools
- **bower**: This is the package manager

Yeoman also provides a generator ecosystem. As per the Yeoman website, "A generator is basically a plugin that can be run with the yo command to scaffold complete projects or their useful parts." So, for example, there are generators for scaffolding an AngularJS, Backbone, or Ember application. The different generators available are listed at http://yeoman.io/generators/.

You can install the Angular generator using the following command:

```
npm install -g generator-angular
```

Once this is installed, there are commands for generating an Angular controller, directive, view, service, and so on. Let's generate a new Angular application now. Make a new directory and cd into it and run the following command:

```
yo angular bookExamples
```

When we run the preceding command, we are asked to choose from several options such as whether we want to use Sass (with Compass) or include Bootstrap, and then we are asked to choose between different modules (as shown in the following screenshot). So you can see the choices I made here (an (*) symbol means you need to include the module, otherwise exclude it):

```
Out of the box I include Bootstrap and some AngularJS recommended modules.

? Would you like to use Sass (with Compass)? No
? Would you like to include Bootstrap? Yes
? Which modules would you like to include?
 ( ) angular-animate.js
 ( ) angular-aria.js
 (*) angular-cookies.js
 (*) angular-resource.js
 ( ) angular-messages.js
 (*) angular-route.js
 ( ) angular-sanitize.js
>( ) angular-touch.js
```

After making our choices, when we press *Enter*, the angular generator generates a directory structure which looks as shown in the following two screenshots. The preceding command also runs bower install and npm install internally (which we can also run separately).

Notice the following important points about the first screenshot:

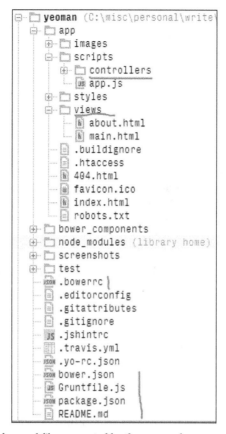

Folders and files generated by the yo angular command.

The root folder has the `app`, `node_modules`, and `test` folders.

The `app` folder has `scripts`, `views`, and `styles` folders.

The `scripts` folder has a `controllers` folder.

The `root` folder also has the `bower.json`, `Gruntfile.js`, and `package.json` files.

Let's look at the contents and purpose of some of the preceding files:

```
{
  "name": "book-examples",
  "version": "0.0.0",
  "dependencies": {
    "angular": "^1.3.0",
    "bootstrap": "^3.2.0",
```

```
      "angular-cookies": "^1.3.0",
      "angular-resource": "^1.3.0",
      "angular-route": "^1.3.0"
    },
    "devDependencies": {
      "angular-mocks": "^1.3.0"
    },
    "appPath": "app",
    "moduleName": "bookExamplesApp"
  }
```

(bower.json)

As you know by now bower is a dependency management tool, so this JSON file
lists all the dependencies under the dependencies key. There are some dependencies
like the one on angular-mocks, which are only required during development (which
we don't ship), so they are grouped under the devDependencies key. Also notice
that the name of the main module is bookExamplesApp as specified by the value
of the moduleName key in the preceding table. Please remember that we ran the
angular-generator using the bookExamples value. Let's check the contents of the
.bowerrc file, as shown in the following code:

```
  {
    "directory": "bower_components"
  }
```

(.bowerrc)

This file specifies the folder where bower dependencies should be placed.
So as shown in the preceding file, the bower dependencies are stored in
the bower_components folder. Let's look at a part of the package.json file:

```
  {
    "name": "bookexamples",
    "version": "0.0.0",
    "dependencies": {},
    "repository": {},
    "devDependencies": {
      "grunt": "^0.4.5",
      "grunt-autoprefixer": "^2.0.0",
      "grunt-contrib-cssmin": "^0.12.0",
      "grunt-contrib-htmlmin": "^0.4.0",
      "grunt-contrib-imagemin": "^0.9.2",
      "grunt-contrib-jshint": "^0.11.0",
      "grunt-contrib-uglify": "^0.7.0",
      "grunt-contrib-watch": "^0.6.1",
```

```
        "grunt-karma": "^0.10.1",
        "grunt-ng-annotate": "^0.9.2",
        "grunt-svgmin": "^2.0.0",
        "jasmine-core": "^2.2.0",
        "karma": "^0.12.31",
        "karma-jasmine": "^0.3.5",
        "karma-phantomjs-launcher": "^0.1.4",
        "load-grunt-tasks": "^3.1.0",
        "time-grunt": "^1.0.0"
    },
    "engines": {
        "node": ">=0.10.0"
    },
    "scripts": {
        "test": "grunt test"
    }
}
```

(`package.json`)

This file again lists `dependencies` and `devDependencies`, and these dependencies are for various npm modules.

> *Bower and NPM are both used for managing dependencies. However,*
> *Bower manages dependencies for the frontend libraries/components (such as*
> *Bootstrap, UnderscoreJS, and so on) whereas NPM does the same for various*
> *Node.js modules.*

Take a look at the second screenshot shown here:

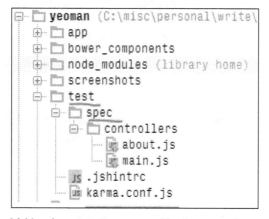

Files and folders for unit testing generated by the yo angular command.

The `root` folder has a `test` folder.

The `test` folder has a `spec` folder, and the `spec` folder has a `controllers` folder.

The `test` folder also has a `karma.conf.js` file. Karma (available at `https://github.com/karma-runner/karma`) is a test runner for JavaScript and can run tests written in Jasmine (available at `http://jasmine.github.io/`), Mocha (`http://mochajs.org/`), and so on.

For any UI application, we can write two types of tests—unit tests and end-to-end (E2E) tests, where the tests actually spin up a UI and interact with it as a user would. For the unit testing Angular code (available at `https://docs.angularjs.org/guide/unit-testing`), we can use any of the existing JS unit test frameworks such as Jasmine, Mocha, and so on. However, for E2E testing (available at `https://docs.angularjs.org/guide/e2e-testing`), Angular recommends Protractor (available at `http://angular.github.io/protractor/#/`), which uses Jasmine for its test syntax. Once we have written the tests, we need a test runner which can run these tests. A good test runner is one which can be configured to run automatically (from continuous integration scripts). So, Karma is the recommended test runner for Angular applications.

Grunt

Grunt is a JavaScript task runner. It automates common tasks such as minification, compilation, linting, unit-testing, and so on. We need to create a task file to instruct the test runner to automatically take care of such mundane tasks.

> *Gulp is described as a streaming build system. It is used as an alternative to Grunt, whereas Grunt relies on configuration over code (meaning the tasks are specified as JSON configuration), Gulp takes the other approach, that is, code over configuration which means various tasks are configured in code.*

It's best to install Grunt CLI (command-line interface) using the following code:

```
npm install -g grunt-cli
```

Now you can run Grunt from any folder and run the following code:

```
grunt --help
```

There's a well-known Unix convention for using command-line arguments by which you can either use the full name of the argument preceded by two dashes - - or by using a single letter abbreviated name of the argument preceded by a single dash -. So the preceding command may also be run as follows:

grunt -h

But not all the command-line applications follow this convention.

Now you'll see that there are many grunt tasks available such as `clean` (for cleaning files and folders), `cssmin` (for minifying CSS), and `htmlmin` (for minifying HTML).

Let's take a look at a part of the `gruntfile.js`, as shown in the following table:

```
grunt.registerTask('serve', 'Compile then start a connect web server',
function (target) {
    if (target === 'dist') {
        return grunt.task.run(['build', 'connect:dist:keepalive']);
    }

    grunt.task.run([
        'clean:server',
        'wiredep',
        'concurrent:server',
        'autoprefixer:server',
        'connect:livereload',
        'watch'
    ]);
});
```

(gruntfile.js)

The preceding file shows a task called `serve`, which is used to run the application. This task compiles the application, starts a web server, and then launches the default browser with the application running. So let's check it out by doing the following action:

grunt serve

Now you'll see an application similar to the one shown in the following screenshot:

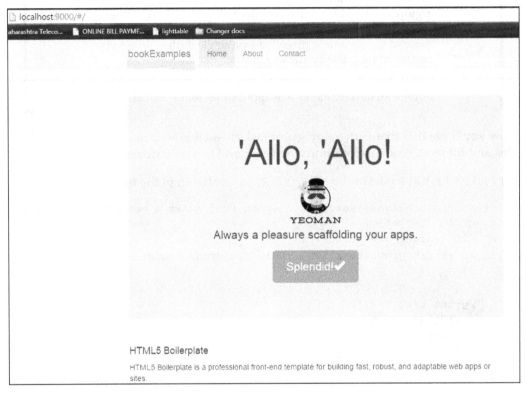

Running application generated by yo angular.

In the preceding screenshot, the name of the application is highlighted; we specified the name of the application as bookExamples when we ran yo angular (as the first argument to this command).

Similarly, the grunt build command minifies the CSS and JS files and updates the references to external libraries from the bower_components folder to their CDN versions, and the grunt test task runs the unit and E2E tests using Karma.

Bower

Just like we use NPM for managing Node.js modules (which are stored in the node_modules folder), we use Bower (available at http://bower.io/) for managing dependencies on the frontend (which are stored in the bower_components folder). Suppose you want to use UnderscoreJS (available at http://underscorejs.org/), you can install it using the following command:

```
bower install underscore
```

This will download underscore in the `bower_components` folder, but it doesn't make changes to the `bower.json` file. However, we want that if any other team member pulls the latest source code, he too should get a copy of underscore on his machine. So we can run the following code:

```
bower install underscore --save
```

This adds an entry for underscore in the `dependencies` section of the `bower.json` file. However, if we want to install it as a dev-dependency, we need to run the following code:

```
bower install underscore --save-dev
```

This adds an entry for underscore in the `devDependencies` section of the `bower.json` file.

 There are certain packages which we need only during development; for example, unit or mock testing libraries or even grunt itself. We don't want to ship any of these to the client. Consequently, both `package.json` and `bower.json` files have dependencies and devDependencies sections. The devDependencies section contains names of packages needed only during development.

B
Git and Git Flow

As some of you might already be aware, Git (available at http://git-scm.com/) is a free and open source **Distributed Version Control System** (**DVCS**). The earlier version control systems such as Subversion, CVS, or Perforce use the client-server architecture in which a server stores the current versions of a project and its history, and clients connect to the server in order to get a complete copy of the project. So the biggest limitation of such a system is quite apparent—you have to be connected to the server to check in or check out any changes. But in a DVCS (like Git), you can check in the changes in your local repository even when you are not connected to the server. Then, at some later time, when the connection to the server is available, any changes made in the local repository can be pushed to the server. So, you can experiment to your heart's content even when you are flying or during your beach vacation.

Now, although there are GUI clients (available at http://git-scm.com/download/gui/linux) for various platforms such as GitHub for Windows (available at https://windows.github.com/), GitHub for Mac (available at https://mac.github.com/), and SourceTree (available at http://www.sourcetreeapp.com/) which runs on both Mac and Windows, the faster way to use Git (and the one which will give you more leverage) is through command line (or terminal) and that is the approach we'll follow here. The biggest advantage of learning Git commands is that these commands are platform independent, so you'll be at home with Git on any OS.

I am using Git for Windows (available at https://msysgit.github.io/) which comes with its own terminal called Git Bash and is integrated with Windows Explorer. Mac and Linux users can type these commands on their local terminal (once Git is installed).

Initial Git setup

Now before we start playing with Git to create repositories and adding/modifying stuff, there are a few things we should do to configure Git for the first time. Once we've done these, we'll hardly modify these settings, though we may if needs be. The first thing we need to do is set up our identity by specifying a username and an e-mail address. This is important because every Git commit uses this information, as shown in the following command:

```
$ git config --global user.name "John Doe"
$ git config --global user.email johndoe@example.com
```

The `global` flag sets this information at machine level, so we need to do this only once (until we need to change it), or we can configure it on a per-project basis by running this command without the global option. We can also configure the editor which will be used while typing a (commit) message. Once we are done configuring it, we can run the following command to check all the settings:

```
$ git config --list
```

Using Git

1. Please check the Git documentation (available at http://git-scm.com/documentation) for a thorough understanding of Git. However, let's see some basic commands on how to use Git (I assume that you have Git installed on your machine). The first step in setting up Git is to create a local folder where you'll be saving your work. So let's say you are writing a book on Angular and you want to show an example of Angular code to your readers, and you decide that you'll keep all the source code examples in a folder called C:\book-examples.

2. So let's open the Git bash on Windows (in the folder C:\book-examples), or on Ubuntu you can open a terminal and type the following command:

   ```
   $ git init
   ```

Once you do that, you'll notice that there is a `.git` folder in your `C:\book-examples` folder:

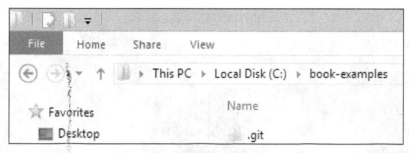

An empty Git repository

Now look at your terminal and it shows you the name of the Git branch as shown in the following screenshot:

```
MINGW32:/C/book-examples                                    _  □  ×

Welcome to Git (version 1.9.2-preview20140411)


Run 'git help git' to display the help index.
Run 'git help <command>' to display help for specific commands.

manoj.waikar@INTH-LAP /C/book-examples
$ git init
Initialized empty Git repository in c:/book-examples/.git/

manoj.waikar@INTH-LAP /C/book-examples (master)
$
```

Git Bash showing the current branch of a Git repository

So as you see (in the preceding screenshot), master is the default branch created, and we can create any number of branches as we want.

Now suppose you add an `index.html` file in the folder. Run the following command:

```
$ git status
```

After running the command, you'll see that you have an untracked file in the local Git repository:

```
MINGW32:/C/book-examples                              _  □  ×
Welcome to Git (version 1.9.4-preview20140611)

Run 'git help git' to display the help index.
Run 'git help <command>' to display help for specific commands.

manoj.waikar@INTH-LAP /C/book-examples (master)
$ git status
On branch master

Initial commit

Untracked files:
  (use "git add <file>..." to include in what will be committed)

        index.html

nothing added to commit but untracked files present (use "git add" to track)

manoj.waikar@INTH-LAP /C/book-examples (master)
$
```

Git Bash showing an untracked file in the repository.

If you look closely, Git also gives you a helpful message to add the file to track.

 Tracking means the file is now being tracked by the Git (VCS), so any changes made to the file are being recorded, and we can see the entire history of changes made to that file.

So, now let's add the file to Git using the following command:

```
$ git add index.html
```

Check the Git status again:

```
$ git status
```

Now you'll see that Git has a newly added file (as shown in the following screenshot):

```
manoj.waikar@INTH-LAP /C/book-examples (master)
$ git status
On branch master

Initial commit

Changes to be committed:
   (use "git rm --cached <file>..." to unstage)

        new file:     index.html


manoj.waikar@INTH-LAP /C/book-examples (master)
$
```

Git Bash showing the newly added file

Now we have to commit this file to Git. When we commit a file to any VCS, we ask the VCS to remember the changes to the file, and the VCS increments the version of the file with the changes in the file. So, let's commit our changes using the following command:

```
$ git commit -m "my first git commit"
```

```
manoj.waikar@INTH-LAP /C/book-examples (master)
$ git commit -m "my first git commit"
[master (root-commit) 05cec81] my first git commit
 1 file changed, 0 insertions(+), 0 deletions(-)
 create mode 100644 index.html

manoj.waikar@INTH-LAP /C/book-examples (master)
$ git status
On branch master
nothing to commit, working directory clean

manoj.waikar@INTH-LAP /C/book-examples (master)
$ git log
commit 05cec8198c3ef985d1f47ccc6d7a7f829d45e412
Author: Manoj Waikar <manoj.waikar@intelliworkspace.com>
Date:   Tue Jul 8 14:20:57 2014 +0530

    my first git commit

manoj.waikar@INTH-LAP /C/book-examples (master)
$
```

Git Bash showing the last commit message

Now, while committing, it's always good practice to enter a commit message describing what changes you have done or what additional code/documentation you are committing. The -m flag stands for the commit message. After committing, if you again check `git status`, you'll notice that you have a clean directory.

A VCS won't be too useful if you are not able to share your changes with the other team members, and that's where the centralized part of the VCS comes into picture; every change made to a system should go into the centralized (remote) repository (if it has to be shared with the team). So to share your changes with the team, you'll have to push your changes to a remote repository using the following command:

```
$ git push origin master
```

Here, origin is an alias for the URL of the remote repository, and master is the branch we are working in. To use this command, we need to set up a remote repository. Please check the section for GitHub and Bitbucket on how to set up a remote repository.

Now, let's see how we can create a new branch in Git. To create a new branch, we've to use the following command:

```
$ git branch bugfix15
```

To switch to that branch, use the following command:

```
$ git checkout bugfix15
```

There is a shortcut for the preceding two commands which is this command:

```
$ git checkout -b bugfix15
```

This command will create a new branch and switch to it at the same time. Please check Git branching (available at `http://git-scm.com/book/en/v2/Git-Branching-Basic-Branching-and-Merging`) for more information about branching and merging. Now let's see why branching and merging are useful.

Using Git flow

Now imagine a very plausible real-life situation where you start working on a new nontrivial feature. Since this feature is nontrivial, imagine you'll take a week to complete it. You start working on the main branch of the project. After a couple of days of work, you still haven't checked in your code yet, because the feature you're working on is not yet complete, and all of a sudden your boss comes and tells you that there is a critical bug which needs to be fixed immediately. Now what do you do? If you are working with a VCS tool like Subversion, you'll probably make a patch, save it somewhere, undo the changes in your main code, and then start working on the bug fix.

> *Keeping your code checked out for long periods of time is not a very good way of working; the recommended way is to check in at short intervals, and if that is unavoidable, then at least check in the changes by the end of the day. So the trick is to work on small chunks of code which can be checked in by the end of the day. This way you can avoid lengthy code merge sessions.*

But this is not true with Git. Git makes branching and merging so easy that there is a much better workflow for the previous scenario; every time you start working on a bug fix or a new feature, you do so in a different branch, and when you are done with the bug fix or the feature, you merge the branch with the develop branch. Now you can do all this branching and merging with Git, but there is a nice little utility called Git flow (available at `https://github.com/nvie/gitflow`), which is perfect for such scenarios and makes these tasks a breeze. Before using Git flow, I suggest you read a successful Git branching model (available at `http://nvie.com/posts/a-successful-git-branching-model/`) by Vincent Driessen. Git flow can be installed by following the instructions available at `https://github.com/nvie/gitflow/wiki/Installation`.

As per the Git flow method of working, we always have two main branches called master (which is used for production releases) and develop (where all development is done). There are other supporting branches such as feature, release, hotfix, and so on. So once you do `git init` on an empty repository, you have to initialize `git flow` in the same repository:

```
$ git flow init
```

This is demonstrated in the following screenshot:

```
manoj.waikar@INTH-LAP /C/book-examples (master)
$ git flow init

Which branch should be used for bringing forth production releases?
   - master
Branch name for production releases: [master]
Branch name for "next release" development: [develop]

How to name your supporting branch prefixes?
Feature branches? [feature/]
Release branches? [release/]
Hotfix branches? [hotfix/]
Support branches? [support/]
Version tag prefix? []

manoj.waikar@INTH-LAP /C/book-examples (develop)
$
```

Git Bash showing the git flow init process

Just keep accepting default values for the questions that `git flow` asks and you'll be good to go. So assuming that your development happens on the develop branch, whenever you have to start working on a new feature, you just have to perform the following action:

```
$ git flow feature start <featurename>
```

Here, `<featurename>` is the name you want to give to your new feature. As soon as you do that, the Git flow makes a new branch called `feature/<featurename>` and switches your repository to the new branch. Once you are done with the new feature and are ready to put this piece of code into action, you can merge your code into the develop branch with the following command:

```
$ git flow feature finish <featurename>
```

Now, `git flow` merges the feature branch's code into the develop branch, deletes this `feature/<featurename>` branch, and switches the repository back to the develop branch, all in one sweet little command.

GitHub and Bitbucket

Now all this while, we have been working exclusively in our local repository. So all our changes are still confined to our own machine. We haven't shared it yet with anyone else in the team. For sharing, we have to push it to a remote repository. You can either have a remote repository on one of your own servers, or you can use one of the hosted solutions; and GitHub (available at `https://github.com/`) and Bitbucket (available at `https://bitbucket.org/`) are two of the widely used free hosted solutions. With the free GitHub option, you can only have public repositories (meaning anyone with access to the Internet can view and download your code). If you want to keep your repositories private, then you'll have to buy one of their paid plans. However, the free version of Bitbucket lets you have private repositories for five users. Here's how you can create a new repository on GitHub (available at `https://help.github.com/articles/create-a-repo/`) or on Bitbucket (available at `https://bitbucket.org/repo/create`).

If you don't want a cloud-based solution, then Atlassian offers a commercial on-premise solution called Stash (available at `https://www.atlassian.com/software/stash`). GitLab (available at `https://about.gitlab.com/`) is another provider which provides commercial hosted and on-premise options.

C
Editors and IDEs

Just like programmers are fussy about their choice of programming language, they are sometimes also very choosy about their choice of an editor or the IDE (Interactive Development Environment). Also, just like it's very difficult to let go of other habits, it's also very difficult to change the habits of sticking to the programming language and the editor/IDE one is used to. The primary reason for this is, of course, the comfort zone one is in while working with familiar tools and techniques. But, as with other things in life, sometimes the payoffs can be huge when one charts an unknown territory. So, I'll recommend you try one of the following editors/IDEs if it is not the one you are accustomed to. You might even come across some treasure!

When we talk of editors, typically the breadth of choices available in the *nix (Unix/Linux/Mac) world are far more than in the Windows world. So, let's start with some of the oldies in this league.

Emacs

Emacs (available at `http://www.gnu.org/software/emacs/`) is the granddaddy of text editors and is probably one of the oldest of all. The beauty of Emacs, however, is that it is one of the most customizable editors out there, so much so that not only can you write code in almost all of the programming languages you can think of but also carry out other activities such as using it as a Twitter client, e-mail client, or a directory editor. Emacs has a **major mode** which tends to be language or task specific (such as Clojure, Ruby, Haskell, Python, and many more), but only one major mode can be active at any given time. A **minor mode** is an optional editing mode that alters the behavior of Emacs in some well-defined way.

Many minor modes can be active at any time, so for example, along with some major mode, the auto-indent minor mode can be active, or we can use the Paredit minor mode (which keeps the parentheses balanced) while working with S-expression based programming languages (such as Clojure, Lisp, and so on). Some of the major advantages of using Emacs are:

- It restricts the usage of mouse to a bare minimum (or none at all) at most times because it has shortcut key combinations for any tasks imaginable. And yes, it is difficult to remember those shortcuts initially, but once you get used to them, your memory can easily recall them even if sometimes you've actually forgotten those. And excellent help is built inside the editor for most of the major/minor modes.

- You'll seldom have to leave the editor because so many modes are available that you can practically do everything from inside the editor.

- It is free, being the baby of Richard Stallman (RMS of the Free Software Foundation (available at `http://www.fsf.org/`) fame)

So, yes, the learning curve is steep and will definitely take some time, but if you learn how to use Emacs, you might not feel the need to use any other editor ever. It is also available for Windows too, so no excuses!

Vim

Vim (available at `http://www.vim.org/`) is the other heavyweight in this category and an old rival to Emacs. So if anyone is talking about Emacs or Vim, the name of the other will invariably crop up. The guiding philosophy behind Vim is again the use of keyboard exclusively, and the biggest advantage of Vim is that it is often available on servers to be used through SSH. So, for example, when you want to deploy something on AWS (Linux) machines, all you'll find on that machine is the omnipresent terminal (the command line) and Vim, so if you are not proficient with both of these, you are going to have a tough time and will most likely have to install a simpler editor like Nano (available at `http://www.nano-editor.org/`) to edit anything. Vim has an **insert mode** where the user enters text and a **command mode** to navigate and edit using keystrokes. Because of a dedicated command mode, Vim has more commands which consist of single keys rather than a key combination. Hence, one can edit faster when one has become accustomed to those commands. Again, Vim also has a steep learning curve but pays you rich dividends because it too supports most of the programming languages, and so you'll hardly need to think about other editors (not to mention that it is also free).

Sublime Text

Sublime Text is cross-platform and more modern than Emacs or Vim, and so will appeal to the majority of users who are more accustomed to IDEs such as Visual Studio or Eclipse. Although it is not a free editor, it has a lot of plugins available through its Package Manager (available at `https://packagecontrol.io/`), which make it suitable for development in any programming language. It is also highly customizable with lots of themes (available at `http://colorsublime.com/`) and other goodies.

Visual Studio and Visual Studio Express

How can one talk of editors and not talk about the de facto standard in the .NET world—Visual Studio (VS, the paid one) and its free counterpart, the Visual Studio Express. The debugging support of VS is one of the best. Before you think about how VS is useful for web development, let me point you to a few extensions such as:

- Web Essentials (available at `http://vswebessentials.com/`), which has support for HTML, CSS, JS, TypeScript, CoffeeScript, and so on

- Node.js tools for Visual Studio (available at `http://nodejstools.codeplex.com/`), which has editing, IntelliSense, and NPM support

- Package IntelliSense (available at `https://visualstudiogallery.msdn.microsoft.com/65748cdb-4087-497e-a394-2e3449c8e61e`), which has NPM and Bower package IntelliSense

- Task Runner Explorer (available at `https://visualstudiogallery.msdn.microsoft.com/8e1b4368-4afb-467a-bc13-9650572db708`), which provides a task runner for Grunt and Gulp directly within VS

The earlier free versions of VS were called VS Express editions, but now they are called the VS Community (available at `https://www.visualstudio.com/en-us/products/visual-studio-community-vs`). It supports coding in C++, Python, and HTML5 (along with Microsoft languages) and for Node.js and JavaScript too. So, this IDE is an excellent choice for people who're already used to VS.

Eclipse

Eclipse (available at `http://eclipse.org/`) is one of the most popular editors for folks from the Java land. Eclipse has a huge community and so many extensions/plugins which can be found on the Eclipse market place (available at `http://marketplace.eclipse.org/`). These can be downloaded and installed from Eclipse without leaving the editor. It has a JavaScript Development Tools plugin (JSDT, available at `https://eclipse.org/webtools/jsdt/`) which helps in the development of JavaScript and web applications. Moreover, it also has plugins for many functional languages such as Erlang (available at `http://erlide.org/`), Haskell (available at `http://eclipsefp.github.io/`), Clojure (which is called Counterclockwise and is available at `http://doc.ccw-ide.org/documentation.html`), and so on, which make it an excellent choice for development in many programming languages.

Now, as this is a book on Angular, I want to talk about two more editors that have extra support for Angular code bases through external plugins. Those are Brackets, which is backed by Adobe, and WebStorm, which is by JetBrains.

Brackets

Brackets (available at `http://brackets.io/`) is a free editor backed by Adobe and has a lot of interesting features such as Inline code editing (where all the CSS selectors that apply to an ID are shown in an inline window by pressing *Command / Ctrl + E*), Live preview (where if you make any changes to your HTML or CSS, you can instantly see those changes on screen), and so on. It too has a lot of useful extensions such as Brackets-Git (available at `https://github.com/zaggino/brackets-git`) which provides Git integration from Brackets, Beautify (available at `https://github.com/drewhamlett/brackets-beautify`) which formats HTML, CSS and JavaScript code, and many others for previewing Markdown, code folding, and so on. The extensions which help in Angular-related coding are shown in the following screenshot:

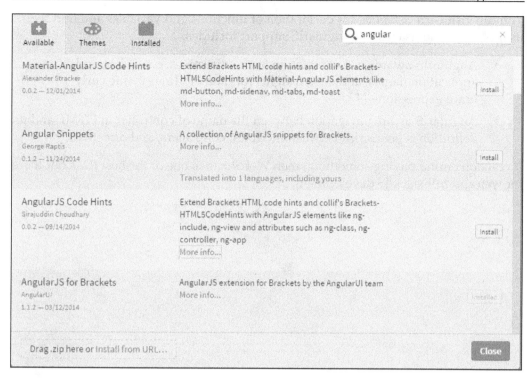

Note that the last one is already installed in my brackets, so the button is disabled; for other extensions, the **Install** button is enabled.

WebStorm

JetBrains (available at https://www.jetbrains.com/) is a well-known company, and they are the creators of the Java IDE called IntelliJ IDEA, the very famous Visual Studio extension called ReSharper (which makes refactoring a breeze), and other tools such as TeamCity which is a Continuous Integration and Deployment server. Now, most of their tools are paid ones (except TeamCity, which has a free version available), and they have one more ace IDE for JavaScript called WebStorm (available at https://www.jetbrains.com/webstorm/). It is a cross-platform editor and has support for most of the modern web technologies such as AngularJS, React, Meteor, ES6, Dart, TypeScript, Node.js, and many more. It has refactoring support for JS code which spans not just a single file but also multiple files.

You can visit *Go to definition* for declaration of functions and variables and find their usages with Find usages. Its AngularJS support includes:

- AngularJS-aware code completion for ng directives, controller, and application names, and code insights for data bindings inside curly brace expressions {{ }}

- AngularJS-aware navigation between the name of controller in HTML and its definition is JavaScript between modules, controllers, and directives.

If you don't mind paying something, then WebStorm is one of the best IDEs out there for web and full-stack JS development.

Index

C

Clojure
  URL 122
cloud computing (Cloud) 52
collection binding 10-12
colorsublime
  URL 121
compilation phase, directive 33
CouchDB
  URL 52
custom attributes 34-36
custom classes
  writing 45
custom elements 36-38

D

data binding
  about 1, 7
  model 7
  UI element 7
data structure
  about 58-60
  data denormalization 60, 61
dependency injection 18-21
dependency management 98
Directive Definition Object (DDO)
  about 32
  URL 33
directives
  about 6-8, 14, 31, 32
  communication between 46-49
  compilation phase 33
  custom classes, writing 45
  defining 32, 33
  DOM, manipulating 45, 46
  normalization 33
  reference link 49
  scopes 34
  transclusion 43, 44
  types 33
  URL 6
  writing 34
directives, writing
  custom attributes 34-36
  custom elements 36-38

isolate scope 38
Distributed Version Control
        System (DVCS) 109
DOM
  manipulating, with directives 45, 46
Domain Specific Language (DSL) 38

E

E2E testing
  URL 104
Eclipse
  about 122
  URL 122
Emacs
  about 119
  advantages 120
  major mode 119
  minor mode 119
  URL 119
Ember
  URL 5
Erlang
  URL 122

F

factory
  versus service 94-96
filters
  about 22-24
  URL 22
Firebase
  about 52, 53
  anonymous authentication 79-94
  benefits 53, 54
  installing 56, 57
  signing up 56
  use cases 54
frameworks
  versus libraries 2, 3
Free Software Foundation
  URL 120

G

generator-angular-fullstack
  URL 28

Git
  setting up 110
  URL 109
  URL, for Windows 109
  using 110-114
Git flow
  references 115
  using 115, 116
GitHub
  about 117
  URL 117
  URL, for Mac 109
  URL, for Windows 109
GitLab
  about 117
  URL 117
Grunt 104-106
Guice
  URL 20
GUI clients
  reference link 109
Gulp 104

H

Handlebars
  URL 4
Haskell
  URL 122

I

implicit annotation 22
installation
  Firebase 56, 57
IntelliJ IDEA 123
Inversion of Control (IoC)
  about 18
  dependencies, injecting 20
Ionic
  URL 6
isolate scope
  @attr option 40, 41
  &attr option 42, 43
  =attr option 39, 40
  about 38

J

Jasmine
  URL 104
JavaScript Development Tools (JSDT)
  URL 122
JetBrains
  about 123
  URL 123
jQuery UI
  URL 46

K

Karma
  URL 104
Knockout
  URL 5

L

Leiningen
  URL 98
libraries
  versus frameworks 2, 3

M

Mocha
  URL 104
Model-View-Whatever (MVW)
      Framework 1
MongoDB
  URL 52

N

Nano
  about 120
  URL 120
Neo4j
  URL 52
ng-annotate tool
  about 22
  URL 22
ngRoute module
  URL 12

TeamCity 123
three-way data binding 74-77
transclusion 43, 44
two-way data binding 1, 9, 10

U

UnderscoreJS
  URL 106
unit testing, AngularJS
  URL 104
Unity
  URL 20
use cases, Firebase
  apps, with Firebase as only backend 54, 55
  apps, with some features powered by Fire-
    base 55
  client and server code,
    powered by Firebase 55
  Firebase API, for your product 56

V

Vim
  about 120
  command mode 120
  insert mode 120

URL 120
Visual Studio 121
Visual Studio Express 121
VS Community
  URL 121

W

Web Essentials
  URL 121
WebStorm
  about 123, 124
  URL 123
Windows Presentation Foundation (WPF) 1

Y

Yeoman
  about 99-104
  URL 99
  URL, for generators 99
Yeoman, tools
  bower 99
  grunt 99
  gulp 99
  yo 99

Thank you for buying
Data-oriented Development with AngularJS

About Packt Publishing

Packt, pronounced 'packed', published its first book, *Mastering phpMyAdmin for Effective MySQL Management*, in April 2004, and subsequently continued to specialize in publishing highly focused books on specific technologies and solutions.

Our books and publications share the experiences of your fellow IT professionals in adapting and customizing today's systems, applications, and frameworks. Our solution-based books give you the knowledge and power to customize the software and technologies you're using to get the job done. Packt books are more specific and less general than the IT books you have seen in the past. Our unique business model allows us to bring you more focused information, giving you more of what you need to know, and less of what you don't.

Packt is a modern yet unique publishing company that focuses on producing quality, cutting-edge books for communities of developers, administrators, and newbies alike. For more information, please visit our website at www.packtpub.com.

About Packt Open Source

In 2010, Packt launched two new brands, Packt Open Source and Packt Enterprise, in order to continue its focus on specialization. This book is part of the Packt Open Source brand, home to books published on software built around open source licenses, and offering information to anybody from advanced developers to budding web designers. The Open Source brand also runs Packt's Open Source Royalty Scheme, by which Packt gives a royalty to each open source project about whose software a book is sold.

Writing for Packt

We welcome all inquiries from people who are interested in authoring. Book proposals should be sent to author@packtpub.com. If your book idea is still at an early stage and you would like to discuss it first before writing a formal book proposal, then please contact us; one of our commissioning editors will get in touch with you.

We're not just looking for published authors; if you have strong technical skills but no writing experience, our experienced editors can help you develop a writing career, or simply get some additional reward for your expertise.

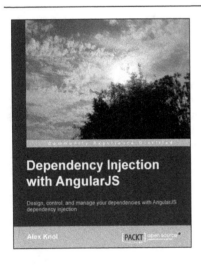

PUBLISHING

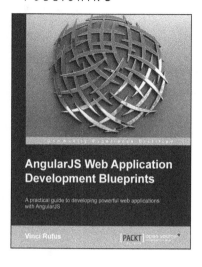

AngularJS Web Application
Development Blueprints

AngularJS Web Application Development Blueprints

ISBN: 978-1-78328-561-7   Paperback: 300 pages

A practical guide to developing powerful web applications with AngularJS

1. Get to grips with AngularJS and the development of single-page web applications.

2. Develop rapid prototypes with ease using Bootstraps Grid system.

3. Complete and in depth tutorials covering many applications.

Mastering AngularJS Directives

Mastering AngularJS Directives

ISBN: 978-1-78398-158-8   Paperback: 210 pages

Develop, maintain, and test production-ready directives for any AngularJS-based application

1. Explore the options available for creating directives, by reviewing detailed explanations and real-world examples.

2. Dissect the life cycle of a directive and understand why they are the base of the AngularJS framework.

3. Discover how to create structured, maintainable, and testable directives through a step-by-step, hands-on approach to AngularJS.

Please check **www.PacktPub.com** for information on our titles